An Insight
into an
Insane Asylum

THE LIBRARY
OF ALABAMA
CLASSICS

Reverend Joseph Camp of Munford, Alabama. Courtesy of The W.S. Hoole Special Collections Library, The University of Alabama. Wade Hall Collection RC506.C3 1882.

An Insight
into an
Insane Asylum

Joseph Camp

With an introduction by
John S. Hughes

And a biographical note on Peter Bryce by
Robert O. Mellown

The University of Alabama Press
Tuscaloosa, Alabama

The University of Alabama Press
Tuscaloosa, Alabama 35487-0380
All rights reserved
Manufactured in the United States of America

∞

The Introduction by John S. Hughes and Biographical Note on Peter Bryce by Robert
O. Mellown are based on articles originally published in Alabama Heritage (Spring
1994).
Library of Congress Cataloging-in-Publication Data

Camp, Joseph, b. 1811.
    An insight into an insane asylum / Joseph Camp ; with an introduction by John S.
Hughes and a biographical note on Peter Bryce by Robert O. Mellown.
    p. ; cm. — (Library of Alabama classics)
    Originally published: [Louisville, Ky.?] : J. Camp, 1882.
    Includes bibliographical references and index.
    ISBN 978-0-8173-5651-4 (pbk. : alk. paper) — ISBN 978-0-8173-8533-0
(electronic) 1. Camp, Joseph, b. 1811—Mental health. 2. Psychiatric hospital
patients—Alabama—Tuscaloosa—Biography. 3. Bryce Hospital (Tuscaloosa, Ala.)
I. Hughes, John S., 1954– II. Title. III. Series: Library of Alabama classics.
    [DNLM: 1. Camp, Joseph, b. 1811. 2. Alabama Insane Hospital (Tuscaloosa,
Ala.) 3. Hospitals, Psychiatric—Alabama—Personal Narratives. 4. Commitment
of Mentally Ill—Alabama—Personal Narratives. 5. Mental Disorders—therapy—
Alabama—Personal Narratives. 6. Patients—Alabama—Personal Narratives. WM
C1835i 1882a]
    RC464.C26 2010
    362.2'10092—dc22
    [B]
                                                        2010020154

To Sarah Pullen Cobbs Camp, my faithful and beloved wife, whose companionship has heightened the joys and solaced the sorrows of forty-seven years; whose untiring service and guiding hand have blessed our twelve children—one of whom is in heaven, and eleven on earth; whose example sheds a sweeter and holier light as the sun of life sinks toward its setting; to her, in fond memory of the past and in assured hope of the future, these leaves from life are affectionately dedicated.

Contents

An Insight

into an

Insane Asylum

INTRODUCTION

By John S. Hughes

$\mathscr{T}$HE trip from Munford in Talladega County to Tuscaloosa had taken two days. Changes of trains in Calera and Birmingham and a carriage ride from the depot in downtown Tuscaloosa had caused the party to arrive at the Alabama Insane Hospital late in the evening. Weariness and expectation affected the travelers differently. While the elderly Reverend Joseph Camp waited outside, Camp's wife of nearly half a century and his son-in-law hurried up the steps and through the front door of the state's largest building. The old man tarried on the grounds in front of the asylum, taking in the impressive, indeed imposing, sight. In particular, he focused his attention on the large fountain located inside the circular drive at the hospital's entrance. In it swam an elegant but artificial swan unlike any the self-educated Methodist minister had encountered in his nearly seventy years of life.

All the surviving evidence suggests that the Reverend Camp was a naïve, kindly man who faced the world with an innocence that belied his advanced years. It seems that his wife and son-in-law counted on precisely those characteristics. As he later explained, it was his wife's idea that, in May 1881, they should journey to Tuscaloosa and visit the well-known and highly respected superintendent of the state's only mental hospital, Dr. Peter Bryce. "[M]y wife said to me, as her health was poor she thought we had better go down to Tuscaloosa and see Dr. Bryce," he recalled. "I agreed, thinking it would be a pleasant trip and a great recreation for my wife, as she is a great home woman."

This was a story, which in substance, Peter Bryce had heard many times. He disapproved of family deceit but could do little about it. Camp's wife, as it turns out, was not concerned about her own health; she and her children were alarmed by her husband's mental state. Evidently convinced that Camp would not have gone to the asylum willingly, she and her son-in-law, a physician, invented the ruse. Only five years earlier, Bryce had explained how he conducted such difficult admissions in his *Annual Report* to the legislature: "It is impressed on [the patient] from the beginning, in the frankest but kindest manner, in the presence of the friends who have brought him here, and perhaps [as in Camp's case] have deceived him, that his mind is disturbed through derangement of his nervous system. . . . Under no circumstances is he ever deceived [once he enters the hospital]."

Bryce was true to his word. After Camp looked over the grounds and the peculiar lifeless swan, he followed his wife into the asylum's administrative hall where he carefully removed his duster and prepared to meet the esteemed doctor. "Pa," Camp remembered his wife saying, "you will have to stay." Bryce then immediately instructed an attendant to take from Camp all his personal belongings: his knife, cane, watch, pipe, tobacco, notepad, and pencil. Camp never said so expressly, but Bryce almost certainly explained these actions and his legal authority to hold him against his will.

What would happen to the Reverend Camp during the next five months and twenty days shocked his simple sensibilities. He was so angered over the loss of his freedom that once he had returned to his family, in November 1881, he composed and published at his own expense the only significant exposé of the Alabama asylum ever written. Entitled *An Insight into an Insane Asylum*, the book provides a rare glimpse into the workings of this important Southern hospital. Much of Camp's account, like the story of his admission, betrays his peculiar gullibility (on which nurses and fellow patients would repeatedly play) and his considerable lack of sophistication. But the book is also remarkably accurate in its reporting of detail. Camp's memory of the physical facilities (even the swan in the fountain) can be corroborated in nearly all cases. His mention of nurses, doctors, and various employees is unfailingly accurate. Even Camp's accounts of the internal practices of Bryce's administration of the asylum comport with official, published accounts and lesser-known archival material from the hospital. In short, most of the descriptive detail of Camp's narrative can be taken as true.

Not every word of his exposé should be considered beyond doubt, however. Clearly Camp's family believed there was reason to commit him—and not just this once. Camp returned to the Alabama Insane Hospital two more times after writing his *Insight into an Insane Asylum*. Records of these later commitments are sketchy. There is no precise record of his second commitment, but in April 1886, hospital files clearly report a *third* admission. His insanity, according to his case history (though not according to him, as we shall see), was rooted in "religious excitement." His own book strongly suggests that he was indeed excitable, though he clearly interpreted religious excitement as a virtue, not madness. Perspective, he might well have argued, makes all the difference.

So while Camp was remarkably accurate in reporting the individual personalities and the events he witnessed, his interpretations, especially the emotional tone of them, should be taken for what they are. Camp was a reasonably prosperous, retired preacher accustomed to a wide range of freedom and respect. Moreover, neighbors and friends likely accorded him some claim to eccentricity. Then, abruptly and without warning, his family's ploy transformed him from an esteemed community elder to an institutional offspring. The adjustment was difficult, indeed bewildering, to this man of great but simple faith. Much of what his alleged exposé attributed to abuse was no doubt rooted in this radical and unwanted transformation.

After learning that he had lost his freedom, he claimed that he "was immediately rushed away and put in a cell without chair, stool, or furniture of any description, without water or any thing save a mattress on the floor and a box in the corner for necessary purposes." This room, as he correctly recalled, was known in the institution as a "cross-hall," a name derived not from any architectural feature, but from the fact that patients placed in such rooms were usually at least "cross," if not enraged or out of control.

Theoretically the cross-hall allowed the patient's anger to dissipate without the use of restraining devices such as straitjackets and without posing physical harm to nurses or fellow patients. New patients, understandably, often fit the description of being uncontrolled. Camp himself was clearly "cross," for according to his own account, he was yelling that he would sue for damages as the attendants ushered him away from his wife and son-in-law.

That long first night, he recalled, was the worst of his life. Through prayer he overcame his anger, gained personal control, and fell into a sort of quiet despair. "I got to crying," he noted, "and never did I feel that I was forsaken by my friends before. I [laid] there and wept until I wanted water." Then, alone in this room, which he described as a "dungeon," he began calling out for water. No one answered his pleas. "I had a very bad cold," Camp remembered, and "could scarcely get my breath when I landed there, and suffered for water and crying for it so long." On later occasions when Camp was placed in the cross-hall, he claimed to have resorted to drinking his own urine.

Camp's experiences in the cross-hall are corroborated by the reports of other patients who never knew him. One, a woman, wrote in 1895 that her fellow patients often cried out for water while in the cross-hall and that she sometimes took water to them when the nurses would not. In 1899, a male patient told a frightening, though uncorroborated, story that Camp certainly would have believed: A man on his ward "begged and begged and prayed in the cross-hall for water. . . . Jackson [a nurse] told me to tell the son of a Bitch to get his own water, he wanted to play cards. [The patient] died that night."

Despite his own fears, Camp did not die that first night but revived, albeit frightened and more tractable, as the staff probably expected, and entered the ward with other inmates. Camp was what was known as a "private" patient in the hospital, meaning that his family, not the state, paid for his upkeep (probably twenty-five dollars per month) and thereby kept him off the "indigent" rolls. As a consequence, he ate at a different table from the majority of patients and received occasional "luxuries" not allowed those maintained at state expense. In any event, perhaps because of his "private" status, he received considerable special attention on his first day. Forney Moore, the nurse in charge of Ward No. 8 ("eighth Alabama, as I called it," Camp remembered), took him on a tour of the grounds and facilities. He saw the "grandest arrangement for cooking [he had] ever seen," as well as "their fine barn, laundry, mill, and water-works."

The only unpleasantness of the tour came when Moore took out his pipe and began to smoke. Camp correctly reported that it was a violation of hospital rules for patients to smoke. But that was not the principal source of Camp's concern. He was convinced that the cause of his alleged insanity was his addiction to tobacco, a habit for which the Methodist preacher admitted to feeling considerable shame. (Tobacco addiction was considered a rare, but not unheard of, cause of insanity in the nineteenth century.) Having been deprived of his pipe since arriving the day before, Camp "was tempted to snatch [Moore's] pipe and run off to take a smoke." But reason prevailed; his station in life—now defined by the previous night in the cross-hall—led Camp to conclude "it [was] best to be subject to the powers that be."

This insight into the wisdom of a prudent subjection to higher powers failed to last, however. Soon after coming to Ward No. 8, Camp witnessed a scene that disturbed him. On Sunday nights, doctors never came onto the wards, and the nurses, most of who lived on the wards with the patients, left their doors open. On one Sunday night, Camp saw the nurses through an open door playing cards in Nurse Moore's room. The sight offended his religious sensibility, and the next morning he reported the incident directly to Bryce and his assistant, Dr. Benjamin L. Wyman, when they appeared for morning rounds. Subsequently, Camp reported, Moore "abused me worse than I ever knew a negro to be abused during the days of slavery." And after that, he and the nurse never got along. Reverend Camp even accused Moore of striking him on several occasions after the incident.

In general, Camp had a low opinion of nurses, such as Moore, who had authority over him. According to census reports for 1880, the average age of the hospital's white male nurses was thirty—younger, that is, than most of Camp's twelve children, and younger indeed than many of his grandchildren. One event in particular highlighted this generational gap. While Camp was taking his midday meal, "in ran a young lad" who said, "Howdy, Grandpa." Camp believed him to be one of his grandchildren who had come for a visit and "asked which of my children's sons was he." The boy answered, "Bennie," which happened to be the name of one of his seven sons. Only later did Camp learn that the "young lad" was actually a newly hired nurse who was in all likelihood put up to the trick by his senior colleagues.

Other incidents of a similar nature confirmed Camp's low opinion of the nursing corps. While on the "airing court," an enclosure behind the men's wing of the hospital, Camp noticed "a gang of young nurses ripping and tearing over the grounds." He notes, "I don't think there is as rude a set of boys in the State. Of all the profanity and obscene language I had ever heard, they excelled." Camp took the opportunity to lecture the nurses on proper decorum. Although Camp never said so, it is likely that the energetic young nurses found humor in the old, presumably insane, preacher's chastening remarks.

According to Camp's *Insight*, the nurses often played tricks on him. On his first Sunday night in the asylum, for example, nurses on Ward No. 8 told him that "there was a telephone reaching to Bryce's apartment from every room in the asylum, and," Camp confessed, "I knew no better for two weeks." The hospital did have a telephone, installed in 1880, but, according to the 1880 *Annual Report*, the phone simply provided communication with nearby downtown Tuscaloosa. Knowing little about this new technology, Camp took the nurses' bait. Thinking he had a direct line to Bryce's private quarters, the old veteran of late-night camp-meetings preached the night away, hoping to impress the superintendent. On the second Sunday night of his confinement, he "preached till near midnight." He reported, "I became very happy and thought that I had succeeded in converting Dr. Bryce [a devout Episcopalian], for I supposed he had heard every word I said." One can easily imagine the young nurses, standing in the hall outside the patient's room after lock-up, stifling their laughs at the joke's success. The whole incident, it can be surmised, did little to enhance Camp's claims to sanity.

One young nurse from Ward No. 9, a Mr. Nuckles, evidently enjoyed shocking Camp. When the minister asked to be shown the graves of old friends from Talladega County who had died in the hospital, Nuckles agreed to take the old man to the cemetery and point out the graves, which were identified only by number. On the way, Nuckles told the old man stories "of the illicit intercourse he had with women, both white and colored, also how he and another man acted at a camp-meeting the year before with a certain woman." When they reached the graveyard, Nuckles, who evidently had not bothered to look up the proper numbers, directed the preacher to the wrong graves, from which the bewildered Camp took a number of stones "as precious relics." Only later did Dr. Bryce tell him that the nurse had identified the wrong graves and that his relics were of no value.

But not all nurses, Camp noted, were cruel. Camp remembered Nurse Thomas Jones often brought "tea-cakes that his lovely daughter would bake for me, and many were the acts of kindness that he showed me, all of which I will remember as long as I live." One such kindness, he claimed, saved his life. Contrary to his better judgment and custom, Camp drank a cup of buttermilk one day at dinner. On going to the wash-room following the meal, he was so overcome with cramps that he "was drawn almost double." When he screamed in pain, Jones fetched him a "syringe and a bowl of lukewarm water, with a cake of soap." At long last, he reported, repeated enemas succeeded: "my bowels collapsed." Jones then ran and brought Dr. Wyman, who cared for Camp during his recuperation from this dangerous, if indelicate, trial. Jones' brother, Zach, also showed a genuine concern for the old man, sharing his coffee at meals with Camp, when other nurses refused him any. Fond of coffee, Camp considered this small kindness an act of real friendship. Another nurse, an Irish immigrant named Gilland, made Camp a gift of his much-treasured Bible, a King James Version published in London in 1804. Camp briefly lived on Gilland's ward, No. 6, and liked it better than the others. "It was the only ward I was on in which I did not hear the name of God taken in vain," the preacher noted. Camp even told Dr. Bryce that the Irishman should be made "superintendent of all the wards."

Camp's relationship with the doctors at the Insane Hospital was also troubled on occasion, although he had far less contact with the physicians, who left the nurses in charge of the hospital's daily operation. Bryce and his assistant, Wyman, made rounds of the men's wards only twice a week, on Tuesday and Friday mornings. On other days, they visited the women's wards and those of black patients who were segregated from the whites. Often they were accompanied by the steward, W. C. Perkins, and the druggist, E. C. Davis. None of these men seemed to have played on Camp's gullibility, as did the nurses, but his relationship with them was not altogether pleasant.

Camp knew Bryce by reputation before coming to the hospital, and he acknowledged respecting the well-known doctor. But when Bryce deprived Camp of his belongings that first night in the hospital and sent him to the cross-hall, the preacher lost whatever positive view of the superintendent he had previously held. Though his book never says so explicitly, Camp may have known that Bryce diagnosed him as suffering from "religious excitement." Camp may even have considered that the doctor was laboring under a deficiency of just such excitement. What Bryce needed, as Camp saw it, was a religious conversion.

Camp's dislike of Bryce may also have been exacerbated by differences in social class. Evangelical Methodists and liturgical Episcopalians typically populated opposite ends of the social scale in nineteenth-century Alabama, and each group viewed the other suspiciously. Certainly Camp was unhappy when Bryce temporarily denied him chapel privileges after his first visit. At these services, Bryce usually read a Bible chapter and then read a prepared prayer (something Methodists of Camp's stripe typically frowned upon). According to the old minister, he got into trouble during the Bible reading when he "happened to respond 'amen' to a good petition." Confused as to why this should result in a loss of chapel privileges, Camp asked for an explanation from a fellow patient, a former Confederate general, who told him that he should have said "ahmen." Bryce, as an Episcopalian, said the general, preferred the latter pronunciation. Camp then told the general, no doubt with devout earnestness, "I pronounced the word as it was used in the Bible and I believe as the Saviour taught." If this rendition of events is true, clearly the superintendent and his patient had fundamental differences unrelated to matters of the old man's sanity.

The first time the two men met on morning rounds, Camp found further reason to dislike the superintendent. Bryce approached Camp and told him that he understood that the preacher had attended the centennial in Philadelphia in 1876. Camp said he had. Bryce then mentioned that he himself had "traveled all over Europe, Mexico, and Canada." However Bryce intended the remark, Camp regarded it as pretentious, responding that he "had seen men who had traveled over Europe with a spade or stick on their shoulder with a pack of table-cloths and towels." According to Camp, Bryce abruptly ended the conversation and "left with his retinue of officers."

On the doctor's next visit to the ward, the two shared no pleasant amenities. Instead, Camp asked Bryce directly "how he could treat [him] without an examination." According to Camp, Bryce said "he had looked at me," leading the patient to wonder how "he or any one else could tell the internal complaint" by merely looking.

Later, Camp turned the exchange into an opportunity to embarrass Bryce. For many years, it seems, Camp had suffered from hemorrhoids, and a fellow patient, not one of the doctors, treated him for the condition. "Parish Priest," as the man was called, kept a stock of medicines in his room and treated his friends on the ward for their various afflictions. In Camp's case, Parish's therapy worked and the painful condition disappeared. Soon after Camp's recovery, Bryce asked Camp one morning how he was feeling and the minister, perhaps with a sly smile, responded "very well," that Parish Priest had "cured" him of his private ailment. Perplexed, Bryce responded that he had no idea that Camp suffered with hemorrhoids. Camp triumphantly answered, "I thought you had looked at me." Allegedly angered, Bryce ordered the nurse to show him Parish's room, whereupon he "went in and took all his medicines, bottles and everything." Camp indeed regretted upsetting his friend and deliverer, but he greatly enjoyed turning the tables on Bryce.

After these events, which may have served Camp as a leveling experience, Camp and Bryce got along better. Bryce, for example, dismissed the nurse, Forney Moore, who had struck Camp early in his stay at the hospital. On another occasion, at an "entertainment," probably a dance in the amusement

hall, Camp and the doctor sat and talked . . . confidentially for some time."
Bryce also provided Camp with "a little table to eat on" in the ward dining-
room because Camp "could not eat as fast as those who had natural teeth."

In 1882, as he wrote in *Insight*, Camp remembered Bryce with little
bitterness. But his judgment was not altogether flattering and likely
represented the viewpoint of hundreds of his fellow patients, all of whom
were constantly in the presence of nurses but were almost never with a doctor
outside of the brief and highly ritualized morning rounds: "Dr. Bryce," Camp
concluded, "has more power and apparently less to do than any king or
potentate on earth, for all he does is to pass through the various wards twice
a week." Bryce, it should be noted, did much more than this. He lobbied
the legislature, corresponded widely with patients' families and physicians
throughout the state, managed one of the largest fiscal operations in the
South, and continued to stay current in his rapidly changing profession.
Most of these functions, largely managerial in nature, understandably
escaped patients' notice.

Camp had a less divided view of Dr. Wyman, Bryce's assistant, whom
Camp described in rich and remarkably accurate detail. Camp recalled that
Wyman had been employed for only a month or so when he arrived in May
1881, that Wyman had just gotten his medical degree, and that Wyman's
father was a professor at the university located a half-mile from the hospital.
Camp's obvious warm regard for Wyman is echoed in the statements of
other patients who knew him. Members of the asylum's Literary Club,
comprised of patients and staff members, for example, elected Wyman
their president. He presided, the preacher noted, "with great dignity." Camp
further explained: "I cannot fall out with the young doctor. He is one of the
best-looking men I have ever seen, carries himself gracefully before all, and
appears to treat his patients with humanity and respect." On one occasion
when Camp fell asleep in his chair, he tumbled to the floor and broke his
nose. He recalled that young Wyman "came and washed, and pinched up my
nose, and with an adhesive plaster stopped the flow of blood."

Interestingly, Camp's attitudes toward the physicians had little to do with
any sort of therapy, apart from this unfortunate nose-breaking incident or
Wyman's care following the collapse of Camp's bowels. From a twentieth-
century perspective, Camp indeed received nothing that would be called
psychotherapy. Talking therapies, such as that pioneered by Sigmund Freud,
were little known in America before the 1920s. Nineteenth-century insanity

specialists (almost never called "psychiatrists" in the 1880s) relied instead on institutionalization and "moral treatment." Patients undergoing moral treatment seldom had intimate contact with their physicians, who relied instead on the steadying influence of an ordered and unhurried environment in which lines of authority were firmly but gently maintained. In time, such an environmental approach often worked. It removed patients from the causes of their excitement or irritation, alleviated daily stresses (after the sometimes traumatizing initial hospitalization at least), and allowed for rest and nature to work their cure. A chronic problem with moral therapy, as Camp's case suggests, was that insanity often resurfaced soon after the patient left the hospital and returned home to the site of earlier troubles.

Bryce's staff, however, was not entirely non-interventionist. The Alabama Insane Hospital, like many institutions of the late nineteenth century, employed the potent drug hyoscyamine, known more commonly as henbane. Primarily used as a sedative, the drug had anti-spasmodic and analgesic properties as well. Its principal known virtue in 1881 was its reliability in making excited patients sleep. Doctors did not believe that hyoscyamine cured insanity. They believed instead that its calming effects could create the necessary starting point for moral treatment to work, and they recognized, from a managerial standpoint, that hyoscyamine could bring much-needed quiet to often crowded and chaotic wards. Due to the drug's high cost, however, and the difficulty of administering it (by hypodermic injection), it could be used only sparingly.

Bryce and Wyman early and perhaps understandably prescribed the use of hyoscyamine to Camp after he preached through the night—via the wrongly supposed telephone connection—in hopes of converting Bryce from his Episcopal faith. Camp admittedly got "very happy" in the process and probably disrupted everyone on the ward. One can assume that this episode, perhaps begun as a practical joke by the nurses, lost its charm in the early morning hours.

For Camp, the use of hyoscyamine was the worst part of his confinement. Davis, the hospital's druggist, not the doctors, typically administered the injections. Hypodermic syringes had only become a part of medical practice since the Civil War, and the technology was still quite crude, with the syringe resembling a veterinarian's device more than an implement used to inject human beings. Camp described his first injection:

Several stout men came into my room, seized and handcuffed me, and put a broad leather strap around my body to hold my hand. They buckled it so tight that it stopped my breath. . . . I was never so frightened in all my life. I screamed at the top of my voice and so frightened the women who were in hearing that they screamed as though they would go into spasms.

Because most of his readers would not have seen an apparatus of the type that Davis employed, Camp described it for them (quite accurately, it should be noted): "The hypodermic they used was a little syringe made of silver, with a sharp needle-like point, which is hollow. They pushed it into my arm just below the shoulder and injected the poison."

Camp's descriptions of hyoscyamine's clinical effects were equally as detailed and accurate. His mouth became as "dry as a chip." The localized area around the injection felt as if a "hot iron" had been applied. And, as the doctors hoped, the drug never failed to make him sleep. Because the procedure caused considerable physical trauma, Davis injected "one arm one night and the other the next." As a result, Camp's arms were chronically swollen and sore, probably due to infection. The notion of microscopic germs as the cause of infection was just beginning to dawn in the medical practice, and one can assume that Davis' injections were less than sterile. Camp remembered that it hurt to wear his coat and that his skin was "as yellow as a pumpkin."

The hyoscyamine also clouded his mind. One evening after falling asleep under the influence of the drug, Camp claimed that the nurses and druggist "applied the magic lanterns . . . for [he] was told they had one." Such "lanterns" were the nineteenth-century's version of slide projectors, which produced images in a darkened room. It is not clear whether Camp had ever actually seen such a device, but he probably had, given that "magic lantern" shows were occasionally put on for patients in the hospital's amusement hall. But this also may have been an episode, like the one with the telephone, in which the staff deliberately played on Camp's gullibility. If so, it worked. "I saw persons apparently as distinctly as I had ever seen one in my life," Camp explained. "As soon as I would try to take hold of them they would vanish. I saw my wife as plainly as I ever did, but when I tried to embrace her she vanished. . . . It is certainly a great mystery," he concluded. Patients like the lonely, aging preacher must clearly have seemed mad when they reported such fantastic tales from their hours under the influence of this powerful drug. "Be it as it may, I hope never to have the instrument applied to me again," wrote Camp.

Camp never conceded that he must have at least appeared deranged. He did admit that "if any thing on earth will dement a man or woman, I think to incarcerate him so that he can have no exercise and no communication with family or friends will alone derange him." But he never claimed this had happened to him. There was "no doubt in [his] mind that if nine tenths of the inmates of that asylum were released and at their homes at work, they would soon be resorted to health and spirits." Asylums should exist, he decided, only for "maniacs" such as were described in the Bible.

Among his fellow patients, mildly disturbed or biblically maniacal, Camp found both friends and enemies. John Austin, a fellow patient, had gained the trust of the staff. According to Camp, the nurses often left him in charge of other patients. But Camp saw little reason for this trust. Camp recorded that he found Austin to be "the most profane man I had ever met. Of all the filthy talk I ever heard he excelled all, and was the worst rake." Perhaps playing on the preacher's self-righteousness, Austin chided him for being a hypocrite. Worse, Austin sometimes lost his temper and "would kick and cuff" the old man.

Austin was untypical of patients, however. Camp evidently enjoyed people, and perhaps his years of ministering to their needs made him a good listener. His *Insight* provides small vignettes of fellow patients that suggest he earnestly sought to know who they were, where they had come from, and what special talents their God had given them. Camp, it seems, took not only himself, but others seriously.

Among the more peculiar acquaintances that the aging Methodist preacher made was that of a "Mr. Ryan, a Roman Catholic from Mobile, originally from Ireland." Camp claimed that Ryan believed himself to be the "Holy Ghost and that he was soon to judge the world." Moreover, Ryan had a "perfect hatred" for Protestants, whom he called "heretics, and would . . . destroy the last one if he were able to do so." In other circumstances, it might be assumed that Ryan and Camp would have been much at odds. But despite his anti-Reformation bent, the devout Catholic actually showed the Methodist preacher considerable kindness. Because Ryan was a "large and portly" man, he received double rations at all meals, as did another Catholic on the ward, a former sailor who worked manually on the grounds every day.

Ryan feared that the slim and elderly Camp was getting too little to eat, and secretly slipped him part of his and his co-religionist's extra portions. "But for Ryan," Camp said, "I do not know how I could have lived . . ."

Most modern readers who come across Camp's *Insight into an Insane Asylum* feel the pull of temptation. Inevitably they ask whether the old man was crazy or not—a question the historian cannot easily answer and probably should not try. The individual facts of his case add up to a puzzling sum: His family clearly thought he was mad; his doctors, too, found evidence to hold him, not just once, but twice more, before the decade was out; but his book, while a powerful testament to peculiarity, offers no clear "proof" of madness. If anything, *Insight* suggests that the line between sanity and madness was blurred at best, and that to define that line requires that we be a part of the social context in which the individual lived. Sanity simply may not have meant to post-Reconstruction Alabamians what it means to us today.

A second temptation, nearly as seductive, is to judge Camp's keepers. Were they humanitarian or cruel? Was the asylum a good or bad place? Such dichotomous questions are always misleading and ahistorical. All persons and institutions are more complicated and contradictory than such labels allow. We today can no more determine conclusively the humanity of the asylum than we can judge categorically the Reverend Camp's state of mind. But being human, modern readers typically yearn for a subtext of melodrama; popular culture has taught us to seek villains and heroes in stories such as Camp's. In this regard, the *Insight into an Insane Asylum* provides an instructive lesson. It shows us that the keepers of mental patients, like the inmates themselves, were abundantly capable of humanity—covering its wide range from generosity to mean-spiritedness. Doctors, nurses, patients, and their families all emerge from Camp's peculiar *Insight* as the complex and often confused creatures they must have been. In the final analysis, Camp's exposé exposes not so much the abuse that he believed it chronicled as the rich range of behaviors demonstrated by people under stress. Life in the asylum was not melodrama; it was real.

CHAPTER I

$\mathcal{T}$HE author of the following work is the son of Joseph Camp, Sr., who was the son of Benjamin Camp, of Virginia, who was the youngest child of twelve children of his father's first marriage — eleven sons and one daughter. By his father's second marriage there were also eleven sons and one daughter, making in all twenty-two sons and two daughters; and what is more remarkable they lived to be grown and had families; and it was published in the *Christian Advocate and Journal* that they met at their father's house with their families and had a great camp-meeting. A daughter of Nathan Camp (one of my grandfather's brothers) bore twenty-two children, among them Virgil A. Stewart, who detected and captured the great western land-pirate, John A. Murrel. Stewart was a son of her second marriage. The name of her first husband was Gideon; the name of her third was Howard. My father at his death had three hundred and sixteen children, grandchildren, and great-, great-grandchildren, and he had the youngest child of all, it being only sixteen days old, and an only child of his second marriage.

I was born August 2, 1811, in Jackson County, Georgia, within two miles of the Appalachie River, the boundary between the Indians and whites. My father was a native Virginian. When grown he and his father and three uncles, John, Nathan, and Thomas, emigrated to South Carolina and settled in Greenville and Laurens Districts, where my father married Elizabeth Camp, a second cousin, who was born in North Carolina, and who with her father moved from Rutherford County, North Carolina, to Laurens, South Carolina. In the year 1799 my father moved to Jackson County, Georgia, and settled with his father and uncles near the Appalachie. My mother had seven sons before she had a daughter; I was the seventh son.

I remember distinctly a circumstance that occurred when I was but eighteen months old. The Indians were very troublesome, and it became necessary to build forts for the protection of the women and children. My only sister living, Mrs. Nelson, who lives in Claiborne Parish, Louisiana, born in 1813, the eighth child, was then but three days old, and it was reported the Indians were murdering the whites near by. My father placed my mother with her small children and bedding in a truck-wagon, and we were driven by my brother Benjamin, now Colonel Benjamin Camp, of Campbell County, Georgia, to the nearest fort, about two miles distant. As we started we had to go down quite a hill, and the team made an effort to run, which alarmed my mother, and that frightened me nearly to death. I remember it as distinctly as if it occurred yesterday, though I was but eighteen months old.

My original family belonged to the Baptist Church. My father and one of his cousins, Hosea Camp, who was the son of Nathan Camp, Sr., were the first of the name that ever joined the Methodist Church. Hosea also moved from Virginia, and was educated for a lawyer. When young he advocated the doctrine of the Universalists publicly, mainly for argument's sake, until he believed it firmly, he told me. Afterward he was converted and made an able minister in the Methodist Church. He lived to great age and died a triumphant death. My father was also converted and became an official member of the church. At my earliest recollection he held family prayers; always standing up to sing before prayer morning and evening. He was very punctual in his secret devotions. I remember well he had his closet in an old workshop that stood near the dwelling where he had his daily prayers. I remember on one occasion, about dusk, I heard a noise in the shop and drew near to see what it was, and found father at prayer. Our house was the preachers' home, it being in the corner of three circuits, each of which was served by two preachers annually. The Presiding Elder, in passing to his quarterly meetings, generally staid with us. At that time Georgia and South Carolina were one conference.

I was convicted of sin at an early day, and was converted in my fourteenth year at a camp-meeting near Monroe, Walton County, Ga. I think my elder brothers were converted and joined the church before this at the same camp-ground. My eldest brother, Benjamin, Walter T. Colquit (the father of the present Governor of Georgia), and Dr. Palmer were converted at the same camp-ground, in the same altar, and at the same time the year before, which was 1824. On the first Monday morning in October, 1825, I joined the Methodist Church, while Isaac Oslin was on the Appalachie circuit, giving him my hand and my name.

I was fond of waiting on the preachers; would ride their horses to water; and among my earliest recollections was when I had been watering their horses and put them in the stables they took me to a pile of straw that lay before the barn-door and prayed for me, laying their hands on my head. I had impressions to preach at a very early age. I had selected a place for secret prayer in our barn. Every evening after feeding the stock I would open the barn-door and spend a long while in crying and praying to God, and often have I gone to the house praising God. I always had a time set in the future when I would take up the cross, offering as an excuse that I was too ignorant, and for the want of an education I would procrastinate going into work until long after I had a family; and I think so long as the devil can get any one to defer taking up any cross for a more favorable time he has a "bill of sale." I thought I was too ignorant, and for want of an education I deferred it, often wishing to warn sinners; but the enemy would meet me and tell me, or suggest, you have no authority to exercise, and I would allow this to be an excuse. Finally I obtained license to exhort and preach; was licensed by Ebenezer Hearn while on the Talladega District. After I obtained license the enemy would meet me and suggest that I now had authority to preach and could not do it. He has often used this argument since, and I fear will follow me to the grave with it. I find the text in Ecclesiastes, "Whatsoever thy hand findeth to do, do it with thy might," is the only safe plan. I have after a way been trying to preach for forty years or more, all the while as a local preacher, though I was employed by Willis D. Mathews, Presiding Elder of Talladega District, to serve the colored mission two years, and the happiest portion of my life was while I tried to preach to the slaves. I was also employed by W. R. Kirk, while on the same district, to serve the Blue Mountain Mission, which was also a pleasant part of my life.

Having a very large family, seven sons and six daughters, to raise and educate, I had to work very hard to do so. My children are now nearly all grown and some are married. My daughters are all married; two of them (one now dead) to members of the North Alabama Conference.

I was ordained Deacon in Talladega in 1854 by Bishop Andrew, also Elder in Eufaula in 1859 by Bishop Kavanaugh, and though I am vested with authority to use all the ordinances of the Church, I feel that I am less than the least of all God's ministers.

CHAPTER II

INSANE HOSPITAL — USE OF TOBACCO — OLD SISTER CARPER —
ATTENDING CONFERENCES — A CONTEMPLATED TRIP — BROTHER
WHITEHEAD — CONSULTING PHYSICIANS — AT THE HOSPITAL — MY
FIRST NIGHT AT THE HOSPITAL

I SHOULD never have thought of writing this work, but for having
been placed in the Insane Hospital of the State of Alabama for the term of
five months and twenty days, for nothing more or less than the use of tobacco,
which I consider as injurious as drinking whisky, and to the constitution I
consider it the greater evil. I contracted the habit of chewing in early life,
by bad associations. Parents who wish to preserve the health and morals of
their children would do well to keep them from all such company, for the old
proverb is true, "Tell me whom you live with, and I will tell you who you are."
I had an old bachelor kinsman who lived with us, that used the weed, and
I being often in his room, would smell the old cavendish. My mouth would
water for the filthy stuff, and finally I would smell, then taste, and at length
would carry it in my pocket until I became a slave, all unknown to my parents.
Thus by degrees I became a sot. After a lapse of perhaps twenty years, I had
the good fortune of becoming acquainted with the Rev. Thomas Scales, a
consecrated man, who professed and lived out the doctrine of sanctification
and preached it on all occasions. I, in company with that good and great
man, Judge Tarrant, went to a two days' meeting in Kentuck to an adjoining
mountainous settlement where Bro. Scales preached against the use of
tobacco. I thought I was converted, and on our return home I mentioned it
to the judge. He told me he was done with the use of the weed. So we pulled
out our tobacco and threw it as far into the woods as we could. Before night
I wanted tobacco, but stood it for about three weeks, when one day as I was
traveling to Talladega (our county-town) I became so addled that I knew not
where I was or where I was going. I had to stop my horse, and consult my
mind several minutes before I could satisfy myself as to where I was. When
I reached home a good old sister Carper was at my house. She told me the

cause of my derangement was the want of tobacco. She gave me her pipe, and told me to smoke a little and it would relieve me of my nervous feelings. I did so, and no old drunkard who had been drinking all his life, and had quit his cup for three weeks, would have been more revived by a dram than I was by a few whiffs of that pipe; so I concluded I would use it a little while, taking a smoke after my meals, until I could wean from it. One day I was lighting the pipe and it fell off the stem on the hearth and broke to pieces, so I thought I would take a small chew, until I could procure another pipe. From that day until the 20th of May, 1881, the day I entered the hospital, I have smoked when convenient and chewed when it was not, until I became so in the habit I could not be satisfied without a pipe or cigar in my mouth. For six months before I went to the hospital, I had the pipe in my mouth nearly all the time, until I fell off in weight from one hundred and eighty to one hundred and thirty pounds. My wife and friends became alarmed.

In December, 1880, I attended the North Georgia Conference. There I learned that my two old widowed aunts were living whom I thought were dead years ago. One of them is ninety years old, the other eighty-eight. I determined I would visit them as soon as I could get things in "ship-shape." In one week after my return our own (the North Alabama) conference was held at Oxford, Alabama, which I attended, and it was my good fortune to be domiciled at that stand-plant of Methodism, Bro. D. P. Gunnel's, where I first met that good and great man, O. P. Fitzgerald, and Bros. Butt, Ripie, Emerson, and Dr. Brown, and where we enjoyed ourselves finely. After my return I worked very hard trying to get my farm in order and crop planted in order to take my contemplated trip to see my two old aunts; and to visit the place where I was born and raised.

In the meanwhile I wrote my brother Benjamin to meet me in Atlanta on Tuesday after the fourth Sabbath in May to accompany me, taking it as an omen that if he would do so, it was my duty to visit my aunts. I wrote him also if he decided to go with me, to make an appointment for us to have a meeting at old Bethlehem on the fifth Sabbath. Brother agreed to do so, and said I must bring with me an old cousin, Rev. Archibald Stroud, who was born the same year I was, 1811, and who lives in the same village. He agreed to go. So we appointed Monday to start; made an appointment to preach in Rome, Ga., at night, and expected to meet my brother in Atlanta Tuesday; but lo and behold! instead of this, I filled a room in the Insane Hospital of Alabama. My family and friends became uneasy about me and said I slept too little, which was a mistake. I sleep six hours in twenty-four, which I consider enough for any man of my age. A female requires something more, seven hours, perhaps. I had several correspondents, and never could read or write with noise about me; so we would have supper and prayers and get our family to bed, then I would write to my correspondents, but would always get my six hours of sleep—enough for me. I never lie in bed awake since reading Mr. Wesley on "Redeeming the time, because the days are evil."

My wife insisted on my going to my son-in-law, Dr. Bailey, early every morning for treatment. This I did for several days before starting to the hospital.

When a Brother Whitehead, from Georgia, traveling agent for the World's Publishing Company, came to my house, wishing to employ me to canvass six counties, to wit, St. Glair, Etowah, Cherokee, Cleburne, Calhoun, and Randolph, we agreed on terms that I considered would be very profitable to me. He handed me the papers giving me the sole right to said counties in the evening. Next morning I was for consummating the trade when he told me my wife was opposed to my taking the agency, stating at the same time that I was demented. I immediately sent for Drs. Bailey, Harrison, and Groce. Bailey and Harrison came and pronounced me sane. Harrison said the medicine I was taking was all right, and told me to follow directions, and I would be all right in a few days.

My wife sent for my life-long friend, the Rev. J. L. Seay, to come and see me. He came that evening and remained until next day, as it is always a treat for us to be together. In the morning my old cousin Archie called. After breakfast I proposed a walk through my farm, which was in nice order, as I had been working very hard to get it in order that I might take my anticipated trip. The exercise of walking caused my medicine to act well, and in my opinion that was the saving clause. I had not taken any thing for years before to act on my liver, and it was very, very torpid. This was Wednesday, and on that day Mr. McKibbon, my son-in-law, came to see me on business. It has always been my disposition never to suspect, and my wife said to me, as her health was poor she thought we had better go down to Tuscaloosa and see Dr. Bryce, superintendent of the hospital, and consult him about our health, and do as he might direct, to which I agreed, thinking it would be a pleasant trip and a great recreation for my wife, as she is a great home woman. Mr. McKibbon said he would accompany us if he had the means to spare. I remarked that I would bear his expenses, to which he agreed.

Upon the Monday previous to our departure, which was on Thursday, I had gone to Talladega to have a summer suit made, but the tailor had so much work on hand he could not make it. I had him to cut it, and brought it home to be made by a tailoress. On my way there I met Dr. Groce, and asked him why he did not come and examine me with the other doctors. He answered that he and one of my sons had attended to it the day before. I could not comprehend his meaning then, but I did the next day. As I was in a hurry I drove on, and left my coat to be made by the time of my return.

At the appointed time, Thursday 2:30 P.M., we left on the S. R. & D. Railroad for Calera, where we staid all night waiting for the train from Montgomery to Birmingham. We waited in Birmingham several hours for the train upon the G. S. Railroad for Tuscaloosa, where we arrived late in the evening of the 20th of May. We procured a hack to convey us to the hospital. When we arrived my wife and son-in-law ran up stairs to the ladies' parlor. I stopped behind to look at a beautiful fountain in front of the building, in the pool of which was the likeness of a great swan floating. I remained some minutes feasting my eyes; at length I went up. Not willing to appear before Dr. Bryce dusty, I asked the porter for the wash-room. I pulled off my duster and washed and combed until they sent for me. My wife stepped up and said, "Pa, did you not say we would come and see Dr. Bryce, and what he thought best for us to do, we would do?" I answered, "Yes." She, crying, said, "Pa, you will have to stay." Bryce told a gentleman to take my knife. I was immediately seized and robbed of my knife, walking-cane, pocket-book, watch, tobacco, pipe, pencil, and every thing. I jumped back and asked, "Why all this? Show your authority and I will submit. If you do not I will sue you for damages, and assess them at five thousand dollars per day, and will not pay a cent for board." He replied he would not charge any thing for board. I was immediately rushed away and put in a cell without chair, stool, or furniture of any description, without water or any thing save a mattress on the floor and a box in the corner for necessary purpose. I suppose they brought me a tin cup of tea, a ration of bread, and a tin plate of molasses, at least this was what they give those who are so unfortunate as to get in the cross-hall, as it is called. I never had such feelings on earth. They brought me a small cup of water which I used for washing my artificial teeth.

My first night in the insane hospital is one that will be remembered by me as long as I live. It was the warmest night I ever experienced, I thought. After being taken to the dungeon I was informed by Mr. Thomas Jones (master of the eighth ward) that General John H. Forney was put there the first night he was incarcerated. I thought I could stand any thing the general could, notwithstanding he is a West-pointer; but I was mistaken, for so soon as I was inclosed I found that in addition to the inner door (which was made so as to admit some light and air), there was an outer door that shut out all. There was but one window in the room and the sash was closed in that, to prevent escape. There were iron grates and a wire shutter, and that was locked to prevent breaking the glass. After I had come to the conclusion of being fast for the night, I tried to compose myself to the situation. I kneeled down and said my prayers. Having finished my prayers, I lay down on the mattress and thought over the past and how my friends had treated me. I got to crying, and never did I feel that I was forsaken by my friends before. I lay and wept until I wanted water. I commenced hollaing for water, water, until my throat became so dry I could not breathe. I called as loud as I could to get some one to go for my wife who was at the hotel, for I knew if she knew how I was suffering she would have me out if she had to blow up the asylum. I first offered one hundred dollars, then a thousand, and ten thousand. I hollaed until my throat became so dry I was about to lose my breath, and I thought I was going to the Judge of all the earth. I had just breath enough to tell them I was dying, and to send me home and tell my friends I was gone to heaven, for I felt God was with me though my friends had forsaken me. Yet all was well. I had a very bad cold, could scarcely get my breath when I landed there, and suffering for water and crying for it so long. I inhaled my lungs full of air and my wind-pipe seemed to close suddenly. I fell to the floor and remained as breathless for ten or fifteen minutes as I will be after this body shall have lain in the grave for a thousand years, and but for having my lungs filled with air and my wind-pipe closed, I never would have written these lines. Struggling for breath, a small vent occurred. I got a little breath and revived, thanks to a merciful Providence. I lay quite insensible nearly the rest of the night.

Chapter III

Becoming Acquainted with the Inmates — Deceptions of the
Officers and Nurses — The First Day — At Prayers with
General John H. Forney — The First Sabbath — Left with
Austin — Card-Playing on the Sabbath — Forney Moore — Mr.
Jones — John Lanthrop — A Maniac — Starving for Water

*N*EXT morning I became acquainted with the inmates of that ward and its keepers, Mr. Thomas Jones and Mr. Forney Moore. They were both very stout men. Mr. Jones said he was a native Tennessean. Mr. Moore said that he was an Alabamian, and that he was raised about Tuscaloosa, if I mistake not, and that he married a Miss Goree, by whom he had several children. For a pastime I began making inquiry about their families. Mr. Moore told me he had no children, and I knew nothing to the contrary for some time. He and Jones lived in the city of Tuscaloosa, and one or the other went home every night. One night Mr. Moore went home and a little son of his had fallen into a well eighty feet deep and was nearly killed. He remained with his family several days, and when he came back and took charge of the eighth ward (eighth Alabama, as I called it). I told him I thought it was a judgment sent upon him for lying to me about his family. But lying was the universal practice of nearly all the officers and nurses. Dr. Bryce himself promised me that I should be discharged the 2nd of August, which was my birthday, and I had received a letter from my wife dated July 11th (the first information I had from the time of my imprisonment), saying Dr. Bryce had written her I was much improved and she hoped the doctor would soon discharge me, that she was raising several turkeys, and that I could come home and enjoy them with her. You do not know how I was elated with the idea of getting home and seeing my dear wife and children. She wished to know if I got any fruit and melons. Though there was an abundance of watermelons, I never tasted one in the year 1881, and but about four apples, and those were given me by the patients. It is true we had a treat or dessert of cantaloupes occasionally that were raised upon the farm, and they were very delicious indeed. I spoke for seed, but as yet have not received them. The doctor promised me that as I wished to celebrate our golden wedding on my birthday (which made my three score and ten, and though we had been married but little over forty-six years, I thought the suffering and privations I had endured entitled me to the remaining four years), that he and Mrs. Bryce would bake the cake, accompany me home, and wait on me. I had written my wife that she must send for Governor Colquit and his wife, as she and the Governor were old schoolmates and the same age, to wait on her. You do not know how delighted I was with the idea of the wedding. I was expecting any quantity of the finest cake, for they are prepared to make it, and they know, or rather the cook does, how to make it. They have the grandest arrangement for cooking I have ever seen. It is so well arranged, they told me, one man could cook for seven or eight hundred persons. But when my birthday came, Dr. Bryce and his good wife left for a watering place in Virginia. I was sadly disappointed, you may be sure.

The first day I spent at the asylum, Mr. Moore went with me on a walk, and showed me their fine barn, laundry, mill, and water-works, but I was in bad plight to enjoy it, for my health was bad and I was deprived of my pipe which I had used for the past forty years. Although it was contrary to the rules for the nurses or patients to smoke, Mr. Moore took out his pipe while we were walking and commenced to smoke. I was tempted to snatch his pipe and run off to take a smoke, but concluded it best to be subject to the powers that be. He at that time treated me very kindly and was quite sociable. At that time I was allowed to go to the diet-table kept by Mr. Friarson, a very nice gentleman indeed. I was allowed to dine with General Forney, who had preceded me there about ten days. I thought as I was put in the cross-hall or dungeon of the general and allowed to dine with him at the same table on No. 1, the first and best table, I supposed I was in the line of succession. On Sabbath morning I was allowed to go to prayers with the general. They have a beautiful chapel. Mrs. Bryce has collected about three or four hundred of Moody and Sankey's best tunes, also those of Bliss, and had them put up in good style. The hymns are not metered but numbered. I think the book contains about two hundred and fifty pages, and such music I never heard. After the hymn the doctor reads a chapter and also reads his prayer. I happened to respond "amen" to a good petition, for which I was excluded from prayers for several days, though not for the first time. While we were at breakfast the general told me I should have said "ahmen." He and the rest of the worshipers, with a few exceptions, belong to the Episcopal Church. I told the general I pronounced the word as it was used in the Bible and I believed as the Savior taught.

My first Sabbath in the hospital I was taken out of my cell and with about two hundred lunatics or patients permitted to take exercise on the grounds, which occupied about two acres inclosed with a brick wall about twenty feet high. The patients were dressed clean and nice. I thought they ought to have preaching. In fact it seemed to me that every day was Sunday. The people were doing nothing and generally well dressed. I inquired if they had preaching; they said not. Every day, with the exception of Sunday, card-playing and every other game was carried on. On one occasion on Sabbath I was not permitted to walk out, but was left with another patient in the eighth ward, whose name was John Austin. He said he was a nephew of Governor Thomas Watts. I do not know whether he was or not. He was the most profane man I had ever met. Of all the filthy talk that I ever heard he excelled all, and was without doubt the worst rake. He cursed me for all the hypocrites in the world.

He was sent with me as a guard to the diet-table, and would kick and cuff me back and forth, and while at the table would tell me if I did not get through eating in five or ten minutes he would make me go back to my ward, and on one occasion in trying to hasten I was swallowing my buttermilk so rapidly that I got strangled and came near losing my breath.

My teeth are artificial, and the under-plate had made a cut into the lower jaw of about one inch in length. I applied to the wardmaster for a knife to trim it off, but was told I could not be allowed to have one, so I had to go about for two months in this condition, and of all the pain I ever felt it was the worst. Chewing on a boil could not have been worse. At length I got the attention of my good friend Thomas Jones, who saved my life without doubt. He trimmed the plate in a minute. You can not imagine what a pleasure it was to eat without excruciating pain.

Austin, with whom I was left alone in the ward, was taken very sick. There was no one to wait on him, so I waited on him as well as I could, and would read the Scriptures to him. We at length became quite friendly. He said one day he would take a smoke and that I must watch for him and not report him. I told him I would do so. We went back to my cross-hall in the cell where I spent my first night, and there he pulled out his pipe and matches and took a smoke. He would send me occasionally to see if any of the officers were coming. Before dinner he fell out with me and cursed me for every thing. I told him that if he did not quit I would report him. He cursed me and said he did not care. Next morning I reported him.

Mr. Forney Moore, Cooper Lee—an old pirate of the high seas who had been sentenced to the penitentiary for some misdemeanor and become insane, and was brought from Wetumpka, the State prison, to the Insane Asylum of Alabama. Mr. Keith, a man of very good heart but badly raised, and a Mr. Leach, a mechanic of the institution, went into Mr. Moore's room and played cards all the evening. The door of the room being left open, I could see them. I also saw Mr. Keith taking a table out of the dining-room and asked him what he was going to do with it. He said they wanted it to play cards on. I reported them to Drs. Bryce and Wyman, a young physician, for which they fell out with me, especially Mr. Forney Moore. He abused me worse than I ever knew any negro to be abused during the days of slavery. He said he was not in the room while they were playing cards, that he was in the hall, while I was certain I walked the hall nearly all the evening and I did not see him out of his room. If he was out, he had no right to let men into his room to play cards on the Sabbath day. From this time until a few days before he left, I had never received such treatment in life, nor have I ever heard of any one that did. Mr. Jones was kind to me; he would bring me tea-cakes that his lovely daughter would bake for me, and many were the acts of kindness he showed me, all of which I will remember as long as I live. On one occasion he invited me to his room and to sit in a chair. I accepted his invitation, for I was not allowed a seat in my own room, and it was quite a luxury to have a split-bottom chair to sit on. In a few minutes he walked out of the room, and in came Forney and picked up a spittoon and struck me on the head, nearly knocking me down, cursing me, and saying Jones would ruin me by showing me so much attention. On another occasion he knocked me down in my room when I was assisting him in carrying the mattresses out of the cross-halls, or dungeons, to put a man in who was a maniac such as the Savior describes in the Gospels, who was in the mountains and in the tombs cutting himself with stones and could not be bound with cords. Without doubt he was one of the stoutest men I have ever seen. It seemed that he could not be tamed, was as active as a squirrel, and had been going on at a dreadful rate. The day before he had taken me for L. M. Wilson, Presiding Elder of the Tuscaloosa District at the time. His name was John Lanthrop. I understood he had been licensed to preach. As

I was his supposed Presiding Elder I could control him generally when he was in the worst tantrums. One day when he was in a dreadful rage, I was in an adjoining room and we could not see each other. I concluded I would try to quiet him. I wish the Presiding Elders of the North Alabama Conference had such influence over their preachers as I, the supposed L. M. Wilson, had over Lanthrop, but I fear they have not, for all I had to do to quiet him was to hiss like a goose, and he would hush instantly, and for doing this to quiet him, Forney knocked me down flat on the floor of the cell. My spectacles flew clear across the room, but fortunately they were not broken.

I nearly famished for water. Six times I was forced to the necessity of drinking my own urine. Twice I could not have lived, in my opinion, one minute longer, but four other times I could perhaps have lived a little while longer. I told Forney if water was not given me I would be under the necessity of drinking my urine, and if so, the world should know it if I lived to get out of that prison; and I feel that I am in duty bound to make it known, though my wife is sitting by and tells me not to write this. The truth ought to be and must be told in all such cases, and I do hope that when the good citizens of Alabama know these facts there will be some laws enacted by which her people may be protected, for there is not a convict in the penitentiary in the United States that has ever received worse treatment than I received in the insane hospital.

Chapter IV

I WAS told by Mr. Perkins that the rule was that when a patient called
or asked for any thing he never received it. Pray tell me, then, how I or
any one else can make my wants known. Mr. Perkins is the corresponding
secretary of the hospital. I was ordered to the cross-hall one day for asking
him please to let me write to my family or to write for me on business of
importance. I had purchased one of the finest colts in the country in May,
but it was too young to be weaned. Mr. Dean, who lives near Alexandria,
Calhoun County, of whom I purchased, was to keep the colt until the first
of July, when I was to send the pay and get it. On the 28th day of July I
happened to think of the matter and asked him to write. It was for this
and this alone that I was immediately ordered to the dungeon. I do not
think any unmarried man should be eligible to be corresponding secretary.
How is he to know of the congeniality that does or should exist between
husband and wife, especially those who have lived together forty or fifty
years, and I told him so. I received but three letters from my family during
the whole time of my imprisonment; two of them from my wife, written
the 11th and 23d of July; the third from my lovely daughter Mrs. Annie
Thornton, written the 13th of July. Though a son who had been absent from
home two years and had returned while I was in prison, wrote to Dr. Bryce
to know if he might visit me, he was not allowed to do so. His business was
such that he was bound to leave before I was released, and I have not yet
seen him. There was no one whom I desired so much to see as he, unless it
was my dear wife, whom I would have given all I was worth to see. I write
this in order to let the citizens of Alabama know how lame are the laws
that govern this institution. Dr. Bryce is the only married man among the
officers. I am told that there is but one man among the officers who is under

bond to the State; yet the lives of hundreds of our husbands, wives, sons, and daughters and thousands of dollars are in their hands. Dr. Bryce has more power and apparently less to do than any king or potentate on earth, for all he does is to pass through the various wards twice a week—Tuesday and Friday mornings at nine o'clock—with his young officers, Wyman the physician, who had just graduated and went there one month before I went, Mr. Perkins the secretary, and Davis the apothecary, who told me he had never been out of the county of Tuscaloosa. Dr. Bryce reviews every Tuesday and Friday morning. On the first review after I arrived at the institution, when he reached the eighth ward, where I was incarcerated, he approached me and said he had heard that I was at the Centennial. I told him I was. He said that he was there also and that he had traveled all over Europe, Mexico, and Canada. I told him I had seen men who had traveled over Europe with a spade or stick on their shoulder with a pack of tablecloths and towels. The doctor then left with his retinue of officers. The next time he passed I asked him how he could treat me without an examination. He answered he had looked at me. I wondered how it was possible by looking at me he or any one else could tell the internal complaint.

About this time General John H. Forney told me that Mr. Parish had cured him of a disease (hemorrhoids) with which I had been afflicted many years. I made application to Parish—Priest Parish we called him—and after taking his treatment two or three times I was much benefited. So the next round after this the doctor asked me how I was getting along. I told him very well; that Priest Parish had cured me. He said he did not know I was affected in that way. I told him I thought he had looked at me. He left and called to the wardmaster to show him into Parish's room. He went in and took all his medicines, bottles and every thing. Parish was hurt with me for telling he had cured me; but before I left he had got a new supply.

I caused quite a sensation one day. It was not convenient for my wardmaster, Mr. Thomas Jones, to go with me to the diet-table, where most of the new patients are fed. Mr. Austin had guarded me there and back and treated me so badly that he had been removed to No. 9. Mr. Jones had brought my dinner on a large waiter. The patients fed from that table were allowed knives and forks. He had carelessly left a long carving-knife on the waiter containing my dinner. I told him I wanted some water, and while he was gone I took the knife and placed it under my mattress. After I had eaten they took out the dishes. Along in the evening I took hold of my butcher and made some demonstrations with it. The news spread that I was in possession of a long knife! Here they came running. I stood at the door. The outer door was open, and there was a little space in the door through which I could put the long blade of the knife and keep them from the bolt or key-hole. They were the worst frightened set of men I have ever seen—about twenty-five of them. Finally they went for a negro nurse by the name of Jesse. He came with a chair drawn back to knock the door down and the cowards were behind him. It reminded me of the Yankees during the war putting the negroes in front when they made a charge on the Confederates. I meant no harm, and rather than they should break the door down, I surrendered. As soon as they opened the door, I threw the knife to them, the point sticking in the floor and breaking off. They were badly plagued.

Upon my first acquaintance with Davis, I inquired the distance to Greensboro. He said he did not know. I told him it could not be further than forty or fifty miles. I spoke of it one day while he was passing with the board of officers through my ward, and soon after he came into my cell and told me that he was mistaken in stating he had not been out of the county; that once he and an elder brother went off from home on a turkey hunt down below Tuscaloosa, and his brother shot a turkey. It flew some distance, fell, and he caught it in Hale County; that he and his brother carried the gun and turkey home. He said that he had also gone away up above to an association of the Baptist Church, and they told him he was out of the county of Tuscaloosa. Yet this Dr. Davis practiced medicine under the direction of Dr. Bryce. He injected into my body the most poisonous medicine known to the profession with a hypodermic syringe. I do not know who did it the first time it was done, for I came so near being killed and scared to death I scarcely knew any thing. It was one afternoon about three o'clock. Several stout men came into my room, seized and handcuffed me, and put a broad leather strap around my body to hold my hands. They buckled it so tight that it stopped my breath, and I was just able to whisper, "loosen it." If it had not been done instantly I should have died. Mr. Forney Moore loosened the strap. I was never so frightened in my life. I screamed at the top of my voice and so frightened the women who were in hearing that they screamed as though they would go into spasms. If I had known what they wanted I would have submitted, which I afterward did. I wish every doctor who uses this medicine as it was used on me had it injected into his body in such doses as were given me. Of all the feelings any one ever had, this was the most painful. I would as soon at any time have my arm cut off as to suffer the effects of this most powerful poison. I am told that it was hyoscyamus, or henbane, and is extracted from a poisonous vegetable and is very costly. But for the cost I think I would have been killed. The physicians told me it was to make me sleep, which I always did. I do not suppose there is a man living of more regular habits than I have. I go to bed at ten o'clock and arise at four. I have followed this so long that I can tell within five minutes of the time, any morning without seeing or hearing a clock or a watch.

The hypodermic they used was a little syringe made of silver, with a sharp needle-like point which is hollow. They pushed it into my arm just below the shoulder and injected the poison. In a minute my mouth was as dry as a chip. I had as soon have a red hot bar of iron applied to my flesh as to suffer this treatment. They put it into one arm one night and the other the next. My arms were so swollen and sore I could scarcely wear my coat, and my skin was as yellow as a pumpkin. It was injected into my arm so near the elbow that I suppose it touched a tendon, and a knot as large as a partridge egg formed and lasted for months. I think there was more of the poison injected into my body than was given to every other patient in the asylum, and this notwithstanding my telling them all the while that I slept enough. I slept as much then as I do now, and as much as any man should at three score and ten. I do not know what would have been the result if it had been continued much longer. I had to have every arrangement made before it was given, for I was as a dead man the rest of the night if it was given at nine o'clock. I remember Davis (or, as I called him, Dr. Friday) gave it to me once with an old dull instrument, and it made quite a sore. The scar is there now.

One Sabbath night I had been to a singing. Davis stopped me in the hall to give me the hypodermic, but I refused, asking him to go into my room and let me prepare. I pulled him along with me, but when I got there I had no light, and had to return to the hall, where there were three lights of gas. I pulled off my coat and he put it into my arm. I broke for my room, threw down the cover, pulled off my clothes, and knelt down to say my prayers beside my couch. I fell asleep and there I lay on the floor the rest of the night. I suppose I turned over on my left side, kicking and struggling with pain. I wore off the skin of my right great toe, also the inside of my right knee. I knew nothing until the next morning when Mr. Rogers opened the door. I found myself lying on the floor all bloody. I applied for salve to heal my wounds. For two months I could scarcely wear my shoe. The scars are there now and I shall carry them to my grave. About this time I read an article in some northern paper giving the experience of an English lady, how she had broken the habit of opium or morphine-eating. A doctor had applied to her for the recipe, and in the article he stated that the hypodermic should be used very sparingly and cautiously, and that no man, unless he understands anatomy well, should be allowed to use it. I wrote an article, quoting from the paper, and wished Bryce to read it, also to take the paper and examine for himself, but he refused. I told him I would not be treated by Davis any longer, that he had nearly killed me.

About this time a maniac was brought to the hospital and Davis, though no physician, came up to give him the hypodermic. It was so painful that he and the two wardmasters, though very stout men, could not hold him still enough to put it into his arm. Davis to prevent his cries stuffed a bed-quilt in and over his mouth. I told Davis he had given it to me the last time, unless he was a better man than I, and I doubted that he was. He never tried it again. I told him it was a scandal and shame to treat a patient in that way, for he did it, I know, in revenge. He threatened me with it one day because I read too loud for his ear. He said if Dr. Bryce instructed him to use the hypodermic, he would do so. I asked him if he told him to kill a man would he do so. He said he would. I told him if Dr. Wyman saw proper to give it to me, he might do so, but as for him (Davis), he should not, nor did he, but the young doctor did. It was in daylight, about the middle of the afternoon, and this was in revenge, I believe, because I objected to Davis's treating me. That evening I think they applied the magic lantern too, for I was told they had one. They applied it also the first time the hypodermic was given me. I saw persons apparently as distinctly as I had ever seen any one in life. As soon as I would try to take hold of them they would vanish. I saw my wife as plainly as I ever did, but when I tried to embrace her she vanished. It was thus with Drs. Goree, Jones, and others. I think the magic lantern the whole secret of the spirit-rappers. It is certainly a great mystery. Be it as it may, I hope never to have the instrument applied to me again. The first time it was administered they gave me two portions, one in the middle of the afternoon, the other at nine o'clock at night. I could not walk. I would see friends on the opposite side of the room, and would try to crawl to them, but just as soon as I was about to embrace them they would vanish. They kept me traveling over the room on my hands and knees until after midnight. Never have I been in such a condition in my life but twice, and then I had taken the hypodermic.

CHAPTER V

*I*N regard to the wardmasters, I can say but little of their morals, out of the eighteen who are employed by the State. I know but little of the females. There are three sisters, Misses Alabama, Georgia, and Florida Duncan, most beautiful and lovely ladies. Miss Alabama is secretary of the literary club, which meets every two weeks. She makes an excellent officer, does her work finely and gracefully. Dr. Wyman is the president. He presides with great dignity and is quite a gentleman, if he did give me the hypodermic. I must say I can not fall out with the young doctor. He is one of the best-looking men I have ever seen, carries himself gracefully before all, and appears to treat his patients with humanity and respect. He is a son of one of the professors in the State University who has been a professor for a great while and stands high in that institution. He was there while Dr. Garland was president. I think the State would do well to continue the young doctor, provided he gets him a wife. I really think the State is in error to have unmarried men look after the welfare of its wives and daughters who are placed in that institution. At least I would not send a wife or daughter of mine there. The club meets every other Monday night. I think they have a ball every Tuesday night for the entertainment of the patients, though frequently others dance, officers and all. I have seen forty on the floor at one time. Every Friday night they have card-playing and all sorts of games— some I had never seen before and hope I never shall again. Though I never knew a card in the deck or struck a billiard-ball with a cue till I went to the asylum, and thought I could never be induced to do so, yet I went into the billiard-room one day, picked up a cue, and struck a ball. It rolled so prettily

I kept on striking until I became quite an expert in the game. It is one of the most fascinating of games. I can account for so much ignorance about the place: the officers and all spend their time playing instead of reading. I told some of them I thought the old proverb true, "Tell me whom you live with, and I will tell you who you are"; that they had lived with fools until they had become fools by absorption. They have singing every Sabbath night, which is the finest entertainment they have. Mrs. Bryce is a fine performer on the organ and one of the best vocalists I have ever heard. She starts all the tunes in the chapel at prayers and in the rotunda at singing. I could not help crying while they sang those beautiful hymns, especially those on pages 154 and 155—the best music in the world, I think. They would sing till the bell rang for nine o'clock, when all present would arise, sing the doxology, and without any benediction leave for their various wards.

One night, not long before I left, while on my way to the rotunda I met with Captain Rucker, a railroad man from Greensboro, who was incarcerated, he said, for not paying the debts of a brother who had failed in business. He told me I must dismiss the society with the benediction that night after the singing of the doxology. I told him I would if I were called on to do so. No one called on me and they started off as usual. Next Sabbath night I was on my way to the singing and met the captain again. He asked me why I did not dismiss the congregation the Sunday night before. I told him because I was not called on to do so. He said he called on me. I replied that I did not hear him. He said Mr. Jones also called on me, and he wished me to do so that night. I said if the officers called on me I would do so, but none of the officers were present. When the bell rang all present arose and sang "Praise God from whom all blessings flow," and I pronounced the benediction. Next morning Mr. Jones told me I was not to go to the rotunda any more. On Tuesday night there was another entertainment at the rotunda. Late in the evening I was in my cell which overlooked the new ward that was going up. I saw Dr. Bryce walking around the building and called to him to know why I was debarred from the rotunda. He said he did not know that I was. I told him that Mr. Perkins had forbid my going because I had dismissed the audience at the singing. He said I should go, and told me to tell my wardmaster to send me. In a few minutes the bell rang for supper. I went to the dining-room and told Jones Dr. Bryce said I must go. He replied that I could not. At that time Davis came around to inspect the table and see if each patient had his rations. Jones told him to see Bryce and ascertain if what I had said was true. After I had eaten my supper, and we had no news from Davis, Jones told me to go to bed, then about sunset. He went with me and locked me in my cell. I told him I would not undress (at this time they allowed me to keep my clothing in my cell), for I thought they would send for me. I waited a while and pulled off my coat and vest. He came and told me to come out and dress and go to the entertainment. I went and met with Dr. Bryce. He was very friendly and sat and talked with me confidentially for some time. He is quite affable. He told me he had dismissed Forney Moore for striking me with the spittoon. I told him nearly all his officers and nurses used more or less profanity. He cited me to two wardmasters present, Friarson and Arnold. I told him I too thought them gentlemen. Captain Friarson is master of the first ward. I boarded at his cro-table a short time after I went there. Next morning as Perkins and Wyman were passing through the wards at nine o'clock they gave me a wonderful blessing for having their order revoked. I asked them who was superintendent, they or Bryce? They replied I had no right to approach Dr. Bryce in their absence. I told them I did not know that they were "chief cooks and bottle-washers" before. Perkins ordered me to the cross-hall and during the day came and abused me with his tongue. He said that I had deceived him. I replied he had deceived me. I knew his relatives, and they were men of the highest type. The Scales family stood at the top of the list among gentlemen. Esquire Scales, who lived and died in Talladega, married a Perkins, whom I supposed was a sister of his father. Thomas Hardin Scales was one of the best friends I ever had. Nicholas P. Scales, his brother, was also a particular friend. They were both Methodist ministers and stood high in their conference, and I thought he was of the same type, but he had deceived me. He left me in my dungeon and went off muttering. It was not long until Dr. Wyman came and was for making peace. I told him I was for peace, and I did not know I had done any thing wrong in asking Bryce why I was kept from the singing. The doctor and I made friends. It was not long until Perkins came and we buried the tomahawk and remained good friends until the last. Though before this I had great reason to complain. He put me in the cross-hall because I walked too fast after him and some lady who was visiting No. 2—the fine ward, and where all visitors are allowed to go. I had just taken my bath in cold water, and was walking for exercise, and happened to walk too near him and his lady. Another time I had been without tobacco for some time. They allowed the patients to chew but not smoke. My wife had sent me some, knowing that I was deprived of my pipe. I asked Mr. Perkins, who kept my tobacco, two or three times to please let me have some, but I did not get any. One day he was some distance off and I called to him for tobacco, but was told when I wanted any thing I must not ask for it. I asked Dr. Bryce how I was to make my wants known. Perkins being present said I must not holla for what I want. I had asked in a low tone of voice several times, but at last hollaed, for which I went to the cross-hall.

My son-in-law, Mr. McKibbon, came to see me, yet I was not allowed to talk with him more than five or ten minutes. He said they told him that company excited me. The truth is I was excited for the want of it. I had a good friend, Rev. Thomas Slaughter, whom my wife had requested to look after me. He visited the place six times before they would permit him to see me; also Rev. L. M. Wilson came to see me but was not admitted.

CHAPTER VI

*M*R. PERKINS is a nice-looking gentleman and I supposed was well educated, until one day when we were in the prison-walls for exercise. There was a gang of young nurses ripping and tearing over the grounds. I don't think there is as rude a set of boys in the State. Of all the profanity and obscene language I had ever heard, they excelled. I commenced to lecture them, when Mr. Perkins rebuked me and asked me some question in Latin, of which I acknowledged I knew nothing, nor even the English grammar, for I never went to a school in my life where it was taught. I told him that I would answer his question by asking him another—would he tell me the meaning of "son of Solon"? (which means a law-maker). He was stumped, and flew into a passion. I was immediately ordered to the cross-hall. He soon came and gave me a wonderful lecture and said I was the greatest bigot he ever knew; that I knew he was not educated, and I did it in company to expose him; that he had never gone to college over three years. I told him he had greatly the advantage of me, as I had not gone to school more than one year and had got what little education I had by absorption. I told him the expression "son of Solon" I got from a circumstance that occurred in Tuscaloosa. It was at the meeting of the first legislature that convened there after the removal of the capital from Cahaba. A gentleman by the name of David Conner was the representative from St. Clair County. He was a man of great natural ability but no learning. He had been an Indian trader, or, as they called them, "sneezers." He was well versed in the Creek language, and while in the legislature a gentleman from Mobile wanted some measure or law passed by which he would be greatly benefited, and he gave the members a large party. Some elegant young lady (and Tuscaloosa at that time had more intellectual ladies than any city in the South, and I suppose North) approached Major Conner and said, "Sir, I suppose you are one of the 'sons of Solon.'" To which the major replied in Indian, "Kitlock stondose," which means in English, "I don't understand you." She ran and told her friends she had met the most highly cultivated gentleman she had ever seen; yet the major could scarcely spell his name. He was one of the first settlers in Talladega and sold goods to the Indians. The place at which he settled is known on the map as Conners; in my neighborhood as the Brick Store.

The first Sabbath night I spent in the asylum I labored under a great mistake. They told me there was a telephone reaching to Bryce's apartment from every room in the asylum, and I knew no better for two weeks. I was not permitted to preach in the chapel nor in the yard, where we were turned out for exercise. So I concluded to preach in my cell. Having a good voice I could be heard all over the ward and nearly over the whole asylum. Mr. Davis was off from home one Sunday night, and on his return he said when near one mile away he heard me distinctly. I remember it well; it was the second Sabbath night I was there. I thought I had gone through all the trials Paul had in Philippi, where he had been thrust into the inner prison for nothing more or less than preaching Jesus and him crucified, and for commanding the unclean spirit of soothsaying or fortune-telling, in the name of Jesus to come out of the servant girl. I selected for my text, "What must I do to be saved? Believe on the Lord Jesus Christ, and thou shalt be saved, and thy house." I preached till near midnight. I became very happy, and thought I had succeeded in converting Dr. Bryce, for I supposed he had heard every word I said. I was sure he would release me. I told Sister Bryce please to treat me as the jailer treated Paul, though it was at this late hour. You remember he believed at that late hour, and was baptized with all his house straightway, and he took them into his house and there sat meat before them. I would be glad if she would give me something to eat and I would start home immediately; would not wait, as Paul did the next morning in Philippi, for them to come and fetch him out openly when they desired to get him out secretly. But Paul was more fortunate than I, at least he left there much sooner than I did, and for my singing and praying I had to suffer in the flesh, and that severely with the hypodermic. If it was given me to make me sleep, it had the contrary effect, for often have I lain awake at night on my mattress expecting the doctor along with it, when I would have been asleep if it were not for fear of his approach. Once or twice I feigned myself asleep when they came into my cell, but they never failed to give it, let my condition be what it might. I was glad when Dr. Bryce told them to stop it.

CHAPTER VII

*I*T seemed that every man—officers, nurses, and all—sought to deceive
me in every way possible. I had formed quite a favorable opinion of Captain
Friarson. He had treated me very kindly and we became quite intimate. He
told me one day that he was going to leave the place and embark in some
other business. I encouraged him to do so, and told him I could put him in a
better business in keeping a flock of sheep and Cashmere goats. He seemed
much pleased with the idea, but before negotiating with him I thought I
would make some inquiry concerning him; so I went to Mr. T. Jones, whom
I thought and still think the best man in the asylum, and asked concerning
Captain Friarson. He said he did not like to talk about his neighbors, but
that Friarson had served a term in the penitentiary, also that I must not tell
any one he had told me about it; then between that and the next day he told
Friarson what he had told me. Next day we were out in the yard, and in the
presence of Jones, Friarson asked me if I had ever heard that he had been
in the penitentiary for cow-stealing and who told me. You may be sure I felt
badly and did not know how to answer him, so I played "shut-mouth," Jones
sniggering all the while, for I had promised not to tell my author. Another
time I was not allowed to go out of my cell for meals. Just at dusk the nurse
had brought my supper and I was sitting on my mattress eating, when in ran
a young lad and said, "Howdy, Grandpa." I asked which of my children's son
was he. He said, Bennie. I had a son by that name. But he ran off, saying he
would be back in a few minutes, that he had driven from Birmingham that
day and must see about his horses. He was one of the nurses in ward No. 9
by the name of Massingale. A patient by the name of Cooper told me he was
his own brother. Another time after Dr. Bryce had deceived me about being

permitted to go home and celebrate my birthday, Mr. Davis came into my room, took up a paper, and wrote on the margin that I would not leave the hospital under five years, unless I was carried to the graveyard, and he the apothecary for the institution. I was promised many walks and took but few; was confined in my cell so long that my feet became so swollen I was fearful I had dropsy, and for exercise have walked around my cell, about ten by twelve feet, as much as five miles a day. I would take off my shoes and walk in one direction—that to the right—until I would become drunk, then turn to the left; by so doing and bathing in cold water I was relieved.

I soon became acquainted with a young man by the name of Nuckles. He told me that Nucklesville, Ga., was named for a relative who settled the place. He seemed quite friendly and wished to get me transferred to his ward, No. 9. He told me he was a Methodist and that he was well acquainted with my good friend Dr. Thomas Slaughter, who, by the way, had requested him to look after my welfare. So he was after me frequently to take a transfer to his ward. About this time for some offense I was removed to No. 6. The principal nurse was an old Irishman by the name of Gilland, with whom I found a Bible. I had gotten one from Mr. Jones when I first went to the place, but it was taken from me in a day or two. Mr. Perkins said it would not do to be religious there, that men could be too religious, which I doubted. Mr. Gilland loaned me his Bible. I soon found it was the first edition of King James, and was published in London in 1804, the first year of that publishing-house, which was the first I suppose in the world, established twelve years before ours, which was the second. This Bible had been taken from London to India by a missionary and brought from there to the United States. It fell into the hands of a Catholic who died in that hall. It was the best paper I have ever seen, also the finest type. The references were not so copious as in some others. I think many are burthened with references and the one hundredth part of them never used, and in such fine print it requires the best eyesight to see them. It was much worn and the lids were sewed on with a waxed thread. About twenty-two of the first chapters of Genesis were lost out. I told Bro. Gilland I wished to purchase it; that I would give him a family Bible worth three dollars if he would let me have it. I desired it as a relic—it had traveled so far, and withal the printing was so well executed, and the references so well arranged, every one pointing to the word or subject. He told me I could have it. I was made up, had got a Bible of my own that I could read at leisure, of which I had plenty, for I had nothing to do; in fact it was the only rest I had ever had since I had been able to work, for I was put to the plow at seven years of age and have followed it more or less ever since until then—seventy years. Bro. Gilland left Ireland in his ninth year, settled in Washington, Wilkes County, Ga., and remained in Georgia until some years since, when he removed to Alabama. I think he told me he followed the jewelry business in Atlanta a while. Now he has a farm not far from Tuscaloosa. He joined the Methodist Church a year or so ago, has been employed as wardmaster in the asylum for some time, and I think the only man in the institution who did his whole duty. He had his patients to wash before meals, and those that were able to get to the dining-room to be there. He saw that each had his full allowance, that they were properly clad, and if any were sick that medicine was brought to them; also he did not allow an oath sworn in his presence. I was with him three or four weeks, and not a word of profane or obscene language did I hear. It was the only ward I was in in which I did not hear the name of God taken in vain. Generally the masters were the worst, especially Mr. Stagers, a nurse of No. 3. He was a very handsome young man and raised in Tuscaloosa. Of all the filthy communications I heard from the wardmasters, he excelled. I was generally the first up and at the bathroom. One morning while on his ward I stepped into the bathroom and found some one lying right where we had to wash. I could not wash without throwing water on him to get him up. He had been to the city the night before and had taken too much of the "over joyful." Had made out to get to the water and there he lay. He had abused me very much, treated me scandalously, so I threw, enough water on him to awaken him. He made out to get to his room. He did not get to the breakfast table. Soon after breakfast the horn blew for the yard. Mr. Stagers and myself had to remain in to keep house. Stagers had gone into the bathroom to take a bath and thus cool off. Some one of the patients in passing out to the yard had bolted the door on the outside. I happened to be passing and saw him reaching over the top of the door trying to unbolt it, but he could not reach it. He asked me to let him out, but I told him I did not put him in and I would not take him out. He begged and plead for God's sake to let him out. I told him I would do so on one condition, and that was that he treat me with some respect and drink no more whisky, to all of which he consented. I of course had to report him, for which he was discharged for a short time, but finally got back before I left and treated me worse than ever. Yet this man has charge of a large number of patients, and is about the character of most of the wardmasters.

One young man from about Cottondale, by the name of Bowen, told me when I first went there that his name was Bowman and that his father was a harness-maker in Talladega. I knew no better for some time. He told me also that he belonged to the Methodist Church, and he thought he could visit a house of ill fame in Tuscaloosa once a week and be a very good Christian. I told him if he did so he would have to repent or go to torment.

Old Bro. Gilland had no such filthy talk. I told Bryce one day he ought to be in charge of every ward with a long whip to prevent so much profanity. He wanted to know how Gilland could keep his patients from swearing. I told him I did not know, unless he did as General Andrew Jackson did — when he gave an order require it to be obeyed. He seemed to wonder that men could be kept from swearing. I told him I thought the next legislature ought to make Gilland chief superintendent of all the wards of the asylum, give him a salary of at least a thousand dollars, and curtail the salaries of some of the others. I think there might be a great improvement in many ways. The institution might be run with fewer men and to better effect. In fact I doubt the advantage of the insane hospital at all, unless for maniacs such as were described by the Savior.

Chapter viii

The First Man Ever in the Asylum — Young Weed, a Patient —
Mr. Parish — Dr. Byron — Dr. Goree — Asking the Blessing
at Table

THERE are men in the asylum as "compos mentis" as Dr. Bryce or any
one else. The first man that was ever placed there was put in on the 6th of
July, 1861, and he is there yet, or was when I left, November 10, 1881. He
is as sane as he ever was or ever will be; is working out of the prison with
others. Perhaps a hundred or so work on the farm under overseers. A young
man from this (Talladega) county by the name of Weed is as well as he
ever was in life. He had charge of the dining-room on No. 8. Mr. Jones told
me he was worth twenty dollars per month. He is a large, stout man and
wants to go home. I offered to give him wages if he could get off and he was
anxious to do so. He is an orphan. I think he was raised by his grandfather.
He became somewhat deranged, while a boy, by dissipation. It is that which
has sent nine tenths of the inmates to that place. He told me he had been
there fourteen years.

Another gentleman was there by the name of Parish, from Montgomery,
who is one of the greatest men naturally and whose acquired ability is not
small. He has been there, I think he told me, fifteen years or more; was sent
there for dissipation while young. He has reformed, does not drink a drop,
reads the Scriptures, sings, and prays regularly, and I think enjoys religion
as much as most men. I learned that he was discharged several years since;
but he thought he was entitled to some damages from the State for the
treatment he received there, and went back on his own account to obtain
some proof, and he says he has been confined there ever since.

There is a Dr. Byron who has been there fourteen years, also a Dr. Goree,
who goes where he pleases. He runs the printing-office and acts as librarian
for the hospital; is as compos mentis as he ever was, and is one of the most
polished gentlemen I have ever seen. Byron had a little of the oddity that I
did not like. On my first visit to the chapel for prayers I took a front seat

so that I might hear. The doctor came in and I was occupying his seat. He told me to move. I did so and took a seat to his right near by. He would turn himself to the right and throw his left leg across his knee, thereby occupying nearly half the seat. Occasionally he would kick me. I at last told him he must quit it. He would throw himself in this position every morning at prayers until I reported him. Dr. Bryce told Davis to move him back; so I felt that I would be rid of that abuse; but the next morning he still occupied the same position and would kick me. While on our way back from prayers I told him if he did not quit it I would kick also. I asked Davis why he had not moved him back. He said he hated to do so, and that I must gain him by love.

It so happened that day we were both moved to the same ward, No. 3. There were so many patients that all could not be seated at the long dining table. About a half dozen of us were sitting around a small round table and the table was set close by or against the wall. Dr. Byron would spread himself as wide as possible, so as to keep me from the table. I was seated by his side and secretly asked a blessing for myself. One day he said to me, just as I had finished, "Don't you ask a blessing or say grace before eating?" I replied I always did, and asked him if I should do it then. He said no, he did not want me to ask a blessing for him. I was just about to do so when he forbade it. He soon finished his ration of lightbread, and as we had grits that day and I did not touch mine, I asked the doctor if he would have it. He thanked me very kindly. I saw that I had gained him with a piece of bread. After breakfast he came to me and asked forgiveness for his bad treatment to me. I told him I would do so if he would that day at the dinner-table call on me to ask a blessing. He said he would. At dinner he could not muster courage to do so, but asked it himself; and that was the last time it was done by the doctor or any one else orally. He professed great friendship for me ever afterward. I left the poor doctor there, as fine-looking a man as I have ever seen, and quite intellectual. I do hope his friends will go after him. His father, who had just died, he told me, was a ruling elder of the Presbyterian Church.

Chapter ix

MR. NUCKLES finally got me to his ward, No. 9. He had for his colleague Mr. Ben Massingale, the youth who said he was my grandson. Before I was transferred I had heard the language of Nuckles and thought it was not such as became a member of the church. I told him I would have to have a certificate from Bro. Slaughter before I could believe he was a member of the Methodist Church. He immediately ran up to his ward and returned with a church-letter, given him by Bro. Slaughter six months previously, as he was going to move away. He held his letter, though not more than two miles away from the church.

A few days after I was transferred to his ward he proposed to walk with me and show me the coal mine, and also the graveyard that I wished to visit, that I might see the grave of one of the best men whom I have ever known, that of Rev. Edward Patton, who died in that hospital. Mr. Nuckles having procured the numbers of the graves I wished to visit, that of Rev. Bro. Patton, 740, and that of D. H. Remson's, of Talladega, 647, we started and passed through the grounds where Dr. Bryce kept his stock. While on our walk he told me of the illicit intercourse he had had with women, both white and colored, also how he and another man acted at a camp-meeting the year before with a certain women. We next went to the coal mine. A large shaft had been dug a considerable depth in the hill rising up from the Warrior River. The coal is hoisted by an engine, dumped into a car, and drawn by two mules on a narrow-gauge railroad. They get coal at this mine for all purposes, both for the engines and gas. All the gas is furnished from these works for the institution, also for the University of the State, located about a half a mile away. On reaching the graveyard we found the numbers on the headboards that we desired, and I was much affected on seeing the grave, as I supposed, of the man with whom I had been associated nearly forty years, whom I had heard preach hundreds of sermons, and also with effect. He was a brother of the late Rev. Samuel Patton, of the Holston Conference, and of John Patton, an able minister, who died in Texas, also of the wife of the Rev. William McLelland, late of Talladega, Ala. A purer spirit I never knew. Though he was nearly all his life a local preacher, he preached as much as or more than any itinerant whom I have ever known. He was a poor man, a wagon-maker. He would work hard all the week, and on Saturday morning would start off sometimes twenty miles to a two days' meeting; would labor hard until Monday morning, then return home to work. Thus he spent his life. I found on the grave most beautiful pebbles of all sorts, sizes, and colors. The whole country around Tuscaloosa is full of them. I gathered some as relics, thinking I would take them home and give them to his friends, and they were many. I took the stones along with me as precious relics, and told my wardmaster to label them and keep them safely until I should get out. I finally came to the conclusion that I would sell them to Bro. Patton's friends and erect a monument over his grave, for he was worthy if any man was. I mentioned it to Dr. Bryce. He objected to its being done there. He said if I wished it done I would have to remove the body. Mr. Perkins told me that Nuckles had given me the wrong numbers; that the numbers were 146 and 20. So I was frustrated in my design.

I asked many times afterward to be allowed to go to the graveyard, but was not permitted again to do so. I fully intended to go and gather some of the stones when I was released, but I was so anxious to get home that I was off in ten minutes after my son and son-in-law came for me. I also intended to remain two or three days and visit my good friends Drs. Guild and Slaughter, Rev. L. M. Wilson, and Thomas Jones's family. I wished to see the young lady that had baked with her own hands the tea-cakes sent to me by her father. I wished to thank her for them. I hope God will reward her, for a cup of cold water given in this way will not lose its reward. May God bless the young lady who will bake sweet cakes and send them to an old local preacher over seventy years old.

Chapter x

*T*HE same evening after our walk to the coal mine and graveyard, Dr.
Wyman informed us my son had come to see me and told Mr. Nuckles as
soon as he could dress me to go with me to the sitting-room. I supposed it
was my son who had been absent so long, and whom I was promised should
come after me. O, I was so rejoiced at the thought of going home with him!

On reaching the room I found it to be my son Eugene. You have no idea
how happy I was to see him and to hear from home. I cried and he cried. He
asked me how I was getting along. I told him as well as I could under the
circumstances, but of all the places for wickedness I had ever seen it beat all;
that I thought it would be more tolerable in the day of judgment for Sodom
and Gomorrah than for that place. I then told him of the conversation Mr.
Nuckles, though a Methodist, had had with me; how he and a Methodist
preacher had acted with a woman on the camp-ground. Dr. Bryce was in the
sitting-room at the same time and heard it also.

Next day Mr. Nuckles went with me and Mr. Aaron Burr Yarborough on
another walk. He told me he wished me to tell Dr. Bryce and Perkins that I
was so excited on meeting with my son the day before that I did not know
what I said or did; that what I said about his conduct was not true. I told
him he had mistaken the man; that I would not tell a lie to shield him or
any other man. From that time he turned against me and abused me in every
way he could. Dr. Bryce had granted me a little table to eat on, as I could
not eat as fast as those who had natural teeth, and said I must be allowed
time to eat.

That night at supper my ration of bread and molasses and a cup of tea was given me. As I had neither spoon, knife, nor fork, I had just clawed out the crumb of a piece of lightbread into my tin plate and had taken the first mouthful, when Mr. Nuckles came up, took my plate and cup of tea, and told me to be off to my room to bed, though it was just sundown. I had to go, but stopped at the wash-room to wash my teeth, and was wiping them on a towel. As he passed he told me to be off immediately, gathered me by my right arm and jerked me with such force from the bath-room that my teeth were thrown clear across the hall and struck the wall on the opposite side. Three of the teeth were broken out and the plate was thus rendered worthless. My teeth were left on the floor, and I thrust into my cell. Next morning he brought my breakfast and also my teeth, and said I must eat in my cell. I asked him to let me wash before I ate. He replied if I could not eat when he brought it, I would have to go without eating, and immediately took my breakfast from me. Not one mouthful did I get from dinner the day before until dinner that day. I was never so hungry in life, and neither water nor tobacco did I get. I asked for water, water, until I told him and Massingale if I did not get water in fifteen minutes I would break the glass out of the window of my cell. Calling loudly I told them I would wait one minute, or until I could count sixty, and began one, two, three, etc., to sixty, then out came a pane of glass.

There were four panes made of pieces of glass. I broke one of these. I then told them I would wait five minutes longer and if water was not given me, I would break another pane. Then I waited one minute longer and began one, two, three, etc., to sixty, and out came another of the pieced panes. Then I told them I would wait another minute and if I did not get water I would break out two; so I began again one, two, three, to sixty, and out I knocked two, which took all but the sound panes.

Then came Nuckles with some or all the officers and took from me all my letters that my wife and daughter had written me, which was all the consolation I had. Mr. Nuckles had furnished me paper and pencil with which to write a history of the hospital. I told him I was going to write a history of the hospital, with all the nurses and patients, and he gave me paper, as he was expecting a fine blow of himself, and would frequently ask me what I was going to say for him. They took several pages of my history, also my Bible I had bought from Bro. Gilland, my pencil, snuff, and every thing. I afterward called on Dr. Bryce for my wife's letters, but I never saw them again. Whether they burned them or not, I can not tell.

About this time Nuckles left and Mr. Massingale was in charge of the ward. It was Sunday and I had nothing to read. They usually furnish the patients with something to read on the Sabbath. A great many papers from all parts of the United States and Europe are furnished the hospital. They have also an excellent library. We were furnished a catalogue of all the volumes, that we might select any work we liked, and through our wardmaster draw every Wednesday. The wardmaster receipted to the librarian. Among the hundreds of papers sent to the asylum was one copy of the *Christian Advocate*, published at Nashville, Tenn., and to me it was the next thing to the Bible. I doubt whether there is another such church-paper published in the world. Mrs. Bryce sent me three *Christian Advocates*, and you can have no idea how much I prized them. One was the Nashville, which gave an account of the Ecumenical Conference in London, the invitation of Mayor McArthur, and the response by Bishop McTyeire. Another was from the M. E. Church North, and the third from Canada. But I think the Bishop "capped the climax." It certainly was the best thing of his life, unless it was his sermon at Huntsville, at the North Alabama Conference, 27th of November last.

I think there should be at least one dozen copies of the *Advocate* sent to the hospital at Tuscaloosa, especially if the paper is prized by others as by myself. The *Christian Herald* and *Signs of the Times* is another paper that ought to be sent there. It is a most valuable paper, published by T. Aitken, New York. I happened to have a copy of it in my pocket when I went there, and but for it I do not know how I would have got along. It answered me for reading matter and also for writing-paper.

CHAPTER XI

WRIT OF *Habeas Corpus* — DR. GUILD — THE MARGIN OF THE *CHRISTIAN HERALD*, AND SPECTACLE-CASE — THE NOTE INTERCEPTED — DAVIS PROSECUTED — NEARLY DEAD — T. JONES SAVED MY LIFE — HUNGER

A FEW days after I went there I concluded I would come out by writ of habeas corpus. I was placed in the extreme west end of the hospital, and through the window of my cell, eighth ward, could overlook the grounds they were preparing for the extension of the building. A white man by the name of Davis with some half dozen negroes were digging out the foundation. They had been digging there for several days. I talked with them through the grates until I got their ear and their sympathy. They promised me they would carry a note to Dr. Guild, an old friend with whom I lodged during the Annual Conference held in Tuscaloosa in 1879, if I could get it to them. So I wrote on the margin of my *Christian Herald* to the doctor, and asked him to see Bros. Slaughter and Wilson and get them to see two attorneys, Powell and Wood, who had been recommended as able lawyers, and get them to come immediately and prosecute for me and bring me out. I prepared my note, but getting it out was the trouble. I found there were two grates, an inner and outer grate, and if I undertook to throw it out and it should strike either and fall on the sill of the window, I could not get it back or forth, as I had nothing with which to reach it. At length I thought of my spectacle-case, which was metal and heavy. I took out my spectacles and placed the note within and closed the case. I then looked to see if there was any one in the yard beside the workmen, and calling their attention, aimed as well as I could to miss the bars of iron. It struck the outer bar and the case opened, but it went with such force that it passed the bars and fell to the ground among the weeds.

Mr. Davis, as all the workmen about the hospital do, carried a key to unlock all the doors of the building. He put the note in the hand of one of his negroes and went with him and let him out. When he returned he told me the boy was gone with my note and spectacle-case. Unfortunately he was intercepted by Dr. Bryce, or some one else. I knew nothing of it for several days, when I learned that Mr. Jones had my spectacle-case. I knew then I was thwarted in my design.

Mr. Davis was removed from his job. I learned he was imprisoned for a while and gave a bond of five hundred dollars for his appearance at court.

I called on Mr. Jones for my spectacle-case and he gave it to me. In the meanwhile the hinge had been broken and Mr. Jones had taken it to the tin-shop and had it repaired. Jones was a kind-hearted man.

But to the other events of my hospital life. In a few days after I went there I had a tin cup of buttermilk given me at dinner, the first I had drunk in many years. I was always fond of it, but it had a tendency to cause cramp. At home I never used it, but having no other I drank it, and had gone into the wash-room, when suddenly I was seized with cramps. I was drawn almost double. I ran to my room and fell on my mattress, and told Mr. Austin, a patient who seemed to have charge to a great degree in the ward, to run for a doctor. He said it was not worth while, that they were all out. I told him for God's sake run for Bryce. He replied it was not worth while for he was with them. I screamed and hollaed. Mr. Jones heard me and ran and obtained a syringe and a bowl of lukewarm water, with a cake of soap, with which I was relieved. If it had not been for Mr. Jones I certainly would have died. I used the bowl full of lukewarm water and filled the bowl the second time with cold water and continued the injections. Finally my bowels collapsed and I thought I would surely die. Mr. Jones ran for Dr. Wyman. He gave me something to stimulate me and I was relieved. Mr. Jones also saved my life by giving me plenty to eat. They gave me blackroot with copperas and salt until I was free from all biliousness, and being weaned from the pipe I had a most ravenous appetite. I did not get half enough to eat and complained to Mr. Jones. He told me to see Perkins and he would give me two rations. He granted it, but for which I believe I should have perished. From that time until now I have had plenty, and better health I never enjoyed. It was the only time in my life that I suffered for something to eat, and it was painful to starve amidst plenty.

I remember one day I had a ration of bread sent me to the cross-hall. It was about the size of my two fingers, made of musty corn meal. I don't think I was ever so hungry before. I was fretted and called for more bread. I was locked up for complaining.

Chapter XII

AFTER I was robbed of my letter and several pages of my history, Mr.
Nuckles kept me confined in my cell and would not let me out. He left the
place for a few days, and, as I have already stated, I was left in the keeping
of young Massingale. He and an old man by the name of Steadmire came
in one day to clean up the cell, which it is the duty of the wardmasters to do
every morning before inspection. Steadmire was a patient, but the patients
have most of the work to do. He is a peculiar old man full of pranks and fun.
I concluded to plague him a little one day while he was in my cell. I stepped
out and turned the key on him. He raved and swore he would pay me back.
I left him locked in while I went to the wash-room, but left the key in the
door and Massingale let him out. Next day Massingale came into my cell
for my plate and cup. I had eaten and put them back as far from the door as
possible. While he went back for the plate and cup I stepped out and locked
him in. He also raved and cursed. I went after water and Steadmire let him
out. They thrust me back with vengeance. They had left a cup in the room
with which I would beat on the door when I wanted water. They demanded
the cup and I refused to give it up. They brought in a man by the name of
Aaron Burr Yarborough, who says he is a son of Aaron Burr. He has all the
shrewdness of Aaron Burr. Steadmire took me by one hand, Massingale by

the other, and Burr by the throat. I thought for a while I would be choked to death. Of course they took my cup.

Soon after I had been placed there, Davis, or Dr. Friday as I called him, would come into my cell, eighth ward, and sit and talk with me, and continued to do so. One day while he and Mr. Jones were sitting carelessly in the cell, through mischief I stepped out and locked them in. I meant no harm, only did it in fun, and to show them their carelessness. Davis did not like it at all. After some weeks he came in and was talking about it. I told him I meant no harm, and to show that I loved him would hug him, and threw my arms around his neck. He pulled his head out of my arms and rushed to the door badly frightened. He left my room for a long while. Jones did not care for it, but Davis never forgave me for putting him in prison.

Mr. Thomas Nee Smith was a singular case. He said he went deranged on purpose. He was quite a young man, lived in Cullman County, had a wife and one child, and was raised in Cullman County, originally Winston. His father and eldest brother had joined the Federal army during the war. His father died in a hospital in Nashville, Tennessee. He had a brother in the asylum, and also a sister had been there, but was then at home still insane. He was brought there some time after I went there. Was put in the eighth ward, where they put all maniacs. He had an open countenance and was a good-looking man. He heard some one call me "parson" and told me he was a Methodist, had been converted two or three years before, prayed in public, and had enjoyed religion, but had backslidden. In the spring before he had let his crop get in the grass, and it kept raining, so he concluded he would go deranged and tried to hang himself. He was the first deranged man I have ever seen who admitted he was deranged. He made a confidant of me. We were placed in adjoining cells and could talk to each other, though we could not see each other. I asked him who was on his circuit? He replied a preacher by the name of Burson. He must be a local preacher, I said. He said no, he belonged to the conference. I then asked who was his presiding elder? He said Parker. I then understood he was a Northern Methodist. Next day he was let out in the hall. I saw he intended getting away if he could and told Jones he had better keep a watch after him. He said he had no fears, that it was impossible for him to get away. It was not long until he found a window where the grate was not well fastened. He tore it away and leaped out. It must have been twenty-five or thirty feet high. He skinned himself badly. Notwithstanding, it took about a half dozen men to catch him. He was immediately locked up in his cell.

Next night he told me he would not be alive in the morning, that he was determined to butt his skull open, that was the only way he could destroy his life. He wished me to ask Jones to put us in the same cell that we might together break the door down and make our escape. He did not mind dying but did not want to be buried there, and wished me to have his body sent home, which I promised to do. One night he said to me he would certainly be dead by or before morning. I told him he would not. "Yes," he said, "he was certain to be a dead man that night." I told him if he died that night I would express his wife seventy-five dollars the next day, and if he were alive he would have to give me a certain fine horse about which he had told me, and which had cost him seventy-five dollars. He said he would do so, and gave me his wife's address. It was not long before the nurses came with medicine for him. I told them the contract and wished them to bear witness. I was soon asleep and awoke about four o'clock. Instead of his annoying me with his conversation as he did every morning, not a word did I hear. I called but got no answer. I came to the conclusion that he was dead sure enough, and feared perhaps I had done wrong in making the bargain I did with him; that perhaps it was the cause or might be the cause of his death. I determined if he were dead to get some one to go to Bro. L. M. Wilson and borrow the money and express to his wife, according to my foolish contract. I believe he tried to die and would have been glad to die. The bell rang and my door was opened. I told Jones I feared Nee Smith was dead. He went into his room and found him alive. I told Jones to write the order for his horse. He denied the contract, and said he was to give me the horse if he died, and if he lived I was to send his wife seventy-five dollars. I told him I was glad he did not belong to the Methodist Church, South. After a while he admitted he had lied in his statement, and said that I should have his fine black horse, called Blake. One day he was let out in the yard for the first time after he broke out, and he gave me an order to his wife for Blake, which was witnessed by two gentlemen who were present. He was handcuffed, and asked me for a knife to cut the handcuffs off. I told Jones if he did not watch Smith would be over the wall. Jones said there was no danger. Just at this moment the horn blew. I put up my papers, order, and pencil, and all parties were moving toward their various wards. I looked around. Nee Smith was gone. I told Jones I could not see Tom, as he was called. At that moment he was seen going over the wall. He had run behind a brick building and got a scantling; had cut off his handcuffs and scaled or leaped the wall. But for a negro nurse who was outside the wall near by he would have made his escape. I think his intention was to get home and run off his horse. He was certainly one of the stoutest men I ever knew. I hope the poor man is well and with his wife and widowed mother.

I never felt so sorry for a man as I did when they locked him in his cell. He cried for his dear little wife and child and old widowed mother. It was heart-rending to hear his cries. One day while we were in the hall he took hold of the iron door or grate at the west end and would have been out in a minute if I had not called for help. He had to be locked in his cell nearly all the time to prevent his escape. He came very near breaking out the grate of the wash-room by punching it with a bench. He got hold of a hammer one day and wanted a young man to go with him to the attendants' room and knock Mr. Jones in the head while he was asleep, get his keys, and make his escape. His whole time was taken up devising plans of escape. Poor man! he had sinned against God and his own body, and no wonder he was in trouble.

Mr. Hall, the wardmaster of the fifth ward, was a very nice man, and I think a member of the Baptist Church. He lived near by the asylum, and on our walks we passed his house. He had a nice family and one of the smartest little boys I ever knew. No doubt he had a good mother. Mr. Zach Jones, brother of Thomas Jones, was the night-watchman for the institution and a member of the Baptist Church. The wives of the brothers were Methodists and there was no doubt about their piety. Zack, as they called him, lost his wife while I was there. She died in the faith, leaving a bright testimony of her acceptance with God. It left a hallowed impression on the heart and mind of her son Obadiah, who was an assistant to his uncle Thomas in the eighth ward. Rev. Mr. Nabours preached her funeral in Tuscaloosa. Zachariah Jones was a liberal spirit. I was for a short time on No. 2, the finest ward in the house. Zack dined at that table. He would give me a cup of coffee every day at dinner. I had been accustomed to having it every meal at my own table and it went very much against my feelings not to get it there. I did not get any while Forney Moore was on eighth ward, but after he was discharged, Tom and Obadiah always gave me a cup out of their allowance, and I fared sumptuously as long as I staid in their ward.

When I first went to the hospital, Mr. Parish, one of the patients, formed quite a friendship for me. My health was very poor and I could not eat one half my rations. He complained of not getting enough, so I gave him one half of mine, for which the old gentleman seemed very grateful and gave me snuff, which he used constantly. I found it very beneficial, as I had catarrh in my left nostril, through which I had not breathed in five years. With the use of snuff and injections of warm water I could soon breathe pretty well; but fortunately, or unfortunately, I got a fall one day that broke my nose. It was one Sabbath evening in summer. I was sitting on a tall seat with my spectacles on and fell asleep. While nodding I leaned too far forward, and off I fell, mashing my nose flat and skinning my eyebrows. I struck a nail, which cut a terrible gash, and there I was bleeding like a hog that had been stuck. They ran for Dr. Wyman, who came and washed, and pinched up my nose, and with an adhesive plaster stopped the flow of blood. My spectacles were not broken. Mr. Parish said I was much improved in appearance, that my nose was too thin, and then it was in better shape; but I did not like the process of gaining beauty. In a few weeks the plaster came off and I was well. I do hope the old man's friends will take him out. He is a coach-maker, and one of the finest workmen in this country. I was told he made the wagons that are used for hauling provisions to the various wards, also the billiard-table on No. 5.

Chapter XIII

The Asylum — The Cattle — Captain Lay's Accounts —
Requested to Perform His Marriage Ceremony — Aaron Burr
Yarborough Again — Mr. Ryan, the Catholic — Cooper Lee —
Transubstantiation of the Bread and Wine — The Priest's Horse,
Bob — Threatened Me with a Spell

*T*HE asylum is situated about two miles northeast of the city of Tuscaloosa, on a beautiful plat of ground, in the midst of oaks and shrubbery. From the city, you enter the ground by a gate so arranged that by striking a piece of iron with the wheel of your vehicle, the gate flies open. It locks after passing through by striking the iron on the opposite side. From the gate, a beautiful gravel walk circles round a lovely fountain of water in front of the main building. This building includes a splendid ladies and gentlemen's parlor, Mrs. Bryce's room, also the room of Mrs. Woodall, the matron, the rotunda, library, amusement hall, chapel, and the cooking department, which is run by steam. I was never permitted to enter this department. The main building is perhaps six or eight hundred feet in length and four stories high, on the top of which is a reservoir which holds thousands of gallons of water. At the extreme north end is the engine and stack, where they manufacture all the gas for the asylum as well as for the State University, which is but a half a mile distant, and a little to the right of the way to the city. The buildings for the patients run east and west from the main building, perhaps a quarter of a mile each way. The males are on the west, the females on the east. This building, including the ground-story, which contains the pipes for the gas, is four stories high. The building on the west end is being extended. I suppose there was one million brick made and put into the wall while I was there. The new building runs square to the right, or due north. It is two stories high and about half done. Mr. Kilgore is general superintendent of all outside business, and a business man he is. He lives on the plantation a quarter of a mile away. He is a man of small stature and has a nice family of children. From my cell, or dungeon, I could overlook the whole new building. It was very interesting to see fifteen or twenty masons all at work with trowel in hand. I know of no other business so exhilarating to me as the building of a brick wall or a new fence. At the extreme east and west ends of the building there are two or three acres of ground inclosed with a brick wall as a place of exercise for the patients. That of males is eighteen or twenty feet high. That of the females twelve or fifteen feet high. They have in the inclosure for the females a few deer which are quite tame. Water is brought from various springs to a reservoir two or three hundred yards distant, which is pumped by an engine to a large tank or cistern on top of the main building. They have a fine grist-mill, planing-mill, and laundry run by the spring or reservoir, beside its supplying water for all cooking, washing, and bathing purposes. They have also the finest stables I have ever seen, which cost, I suppose, not less than four or five thousand dollars each. They have some very good cattle and hogs. The hogs are of the Neapolitan strain, the cattle of various breeds. They have a young cow, I was told, that gave seven gallons of milk per day at seventeen months old. Dr. Bryce told me he had one cow that gave eight gallons. A patient by the name of Captain Lay told me he had a cow in Louisville twenty-two years old, of the Durham stock, that gave sixteen gallons. I told him if he would bring me ten such cows I would give him ten thousand dollars. It was lie who told me of the cow seventeen months old. While taking a walk together one day I saw the cow and doubted the statement about the quantity of milk she was said to give. I told the crowd of gentlemen with us of Lay's Kentucky cow. He said it was his father's. I then said I would have to see her before I could believe she would give sixteen gallons of milk per day. He flew into a passion and would not speak to me for a long time. I think the cows are scarce that give even eight gallons. The captain and I were quite intimate up to the time of this walk. He had taken quite a fancy to a young lady in the asylum and told me they were engaged and would be married very soon, and desired me to perform the ceremony. After I told about his fine cow he had no more use for me and denied saying he was engaged to the young lady. Lay told me he had a large body of land near Mobile, Ala., and that he had a brother recently killed in Rome, Ga., by the turning over of a buggy, who had left him a large fortune. Nearly every demented man I met had a large fortune. One gentleman by the name of Stewart said he had in bank in Arkansas a million millions of dollars and other property besides. He told me when I first went there he was going to take a trip to London soon to the

Ecumenical Conference, and that he would defray my expenses if I would go with him and his family, to which I consented.

Another gentleman, by the name of Aaron Burr Yarborough, whom I have mentioned, is a man of talent. He was born and partly reared in Athens, Alabama, ran away from home in early life, traveled over Europe, and was with Santa Anna and Sam Houston in the battle of San Jacinto. He said that Santa Anna had given him a league of land near the city of Mexico, also that he owns the land on which the Insane Hospital of Alabama is built, and that the deed for the same is in the hands of a gentleman in Tuscaloosa. He had escaped prison several times. Once he went out on the farm to work and feigned himself sick. He let the hands get ahead and then ran to the woods, and thus made his escape. This man is very highly educated and his handwriting is most beautiful. He is now in the prime of life and is indeed a rare person. He was in Pittsburgh, he says, at the time of the strike in 1878, and saw millions' worth of property destroyed.

Mr. Ryan, a Roman Catholic from Mobile, originally from Ireland, is a highly educated and extensively read man. He is large and portly and is about sixty years of age. He hates the Protestants with a perfect hatred; calls them heretics, and would, he says, destroy the last one if he were able to do so. He was a shoe and boot-maker and carried on that business in Mobile; was perfectly sane in every thing except religion. He thought he was the Holy Ghost and that he was soon to judge the world. The time set was 22d of November, 1881. Then he intended giving the heretics their portion in the lake that burns with fire and brimstone. Yet withal he was a kind-hearted man. On account of his size he had double rations given him. At the table he sat opposite another Irishman by the name of Cooper Lee, who was a mattress-maker, and on account of his being a laborer was allowed double rations of bread and meat. He was feeble and could not eat more than half his allowance. I asked him for meat and bread that he left, but he cursed me and would have seen me in purgatory before he would give it to me. He would give what he left to Mr. Ryan and Ryan would slip it to me. By this means I had pretty good fare, at least enough to preserve life. But for Ryan I do not know how I could have lived while in that ward.

After getting through with the hypodermic, black-root, copperas, and salt, I had an excellent appetite. Never did I relish beef, grits, peas, and okra so well before, and I continue to do so. Notwithstanding Mr. Ryan would give me a portion of his own rations and of Cooper Lee's also, he would curse me for a heretic. We could not agree upon his doctrines, especially the sacrament of the Lord's supper. He said the priest, in the consecration of the elements, could or would transubstantiate the bread and wine into the real body and blood of the Savior. I told him a circumstance I had read of a young man in Europe who joined the Catholic Church but could not believe in transubstantiation. He had to travel some distance to get shipping to a foreign country. On his way thither he called on his priest and desired to have the difficulty removed—that of the consecration of the bread and wine into the real body and blood of the Savior. The priest told him to believe it was so and it would be so. He still could not see the point. The next morning when the young man was about to leave, the priest told him to take his fine riding-horse, by the name of Bob, ride to the town of embarkation, and leave him for some one to bring back home. The parishioner concluded to test his doctrine; so he sold the priest's horse and put the money in his own pocket and wrote a note to the reverend father telling him to believe he had received Bob and he would receive him.

Ryan became furious and told me he had put a spell upon a patient in that ward not long before and the patient had died, and that he would put it on me. He half closed his hand, and looking through it said I had but forty days to live. The next day he said I had but thirty-nine; the next, thirty-eight, and the next thirty-seven. Mr. Jones told me the man did die, and I did not wish such remarks to be made about me. So I told Ryan if I should sicken and die I would try and make my will, and I would request in my will that he be prosecuted for murder, and that as he had already acknowledged that he had killed a man, I would not wait to have him prosecuted, but would immediately have him arrested, tried, and hung for murder. He flew into a passion and called for the wardmasters to put me into the cross-hall. He doubled up his fist and I believe he would have jumped on me if I had not left him. I believe I cured him, as I heard no more of his being the Holy Ghost as long as I staid there, and he never spoke to me afterward.

Chapter xiv

*M*R. FORD, another patient, from Cherokee County, Alabama, was another case of the same sort. He was of the order Melchizedek, without beginning of days or end of life. He said he was the eternal Son of God. Upon every other subject he was rational, except he would not claim his wife and children. He said his children were Fords, but they were not his children. He was a man well to do in his county, of fine demeanor, and stood high in his community. Unfortunately he had met with one Sherman, who taught that he and all Christians have power to raise the dead, give sight to the blind, hearing to the deaf, and to cure all manner of disease. He went through all the Hillobee country teaching and preaching this doctrine and had many followers. He quoted Scriptures to prove his assertions— "According to your faith, so be it unto you"; that "all things are possible to him that believeth." He taught that miracles are wrought now as well as in the days of the Savior. He made believers not only of old Bro. Ford but of Bro. Smeley, a good Baptist brother now living in the Hillobees, in the lower part of this (Talladega) county, and also of Demosteler, and many others. Sherman fled from this country to parts unknown, and it is hoped he will never make his appearance again, for he is more dangerous than any Mormon, and they are very dangerous.

Dr. Coleman was from Butler County, and I think a good old man. He has been in the asylum for years. There is no harm in him at all. Talks to himself all the while when alone. There is nothing vicious about him, and no doubt if out of the asylum where he could take exercise would be all right.

The Bible teaches us, "He that worketh not neither shall he eat," and he who violates this law will pay the penalty with dyspepsia, hypochondria, or, which is worse, blues, and there is no doubt in my mind that if nine tenths of the inmates of that asylum were released and at their homes at work, they would soon be restored to health and spirits; for if any thing on earth will dement a man or woman, I think to incarcerate him so that he can have no exercise and no communication with family or friends will alone derange him, and for God's sake, and my soul and body's sake, never let me be put there for the restoration of my mental powers.

I believe asylums, conducted in the manner in which most of them are conducted, are a great curse to the land. They do far more harm than good. The legislatures of the various States would do well to look into this matter. I believe that one ward the size of those in the asylum at Tuscaloosa would be sufficient for every patient, in any State of the Union. No one but a maniac, such as described by the Savior, should be incarcerated. Then let there be a department in all State prisons for such, and let each county take care of all others, with her poor and paupers, and you will save this government millions of dollars annually. What! put an intelligent man or woman in charge of an illiterate man or woman, and often in charge of negro overseers or nurses, and let them beat and knock them over their heads with spittoons and cudgels, throw them down and stuff blankets into their mouths and over their heads to prevent their cries, while having the hypodermic inserted into their bodies! Also to be thrust into bathing-tubs and drowned is not desirable with any patient or friend to humanity. All this I have witnessed and heard, and if any one who reads this believes to the contrary, let him call on Mr. Parish and others of the insane hospital, who will testify to the truth of my statement.

There should be stringent laws enacted for the regulation of all insane hospitals. In the first place, the patients should have humane treatment. No man or woman but those of the purest morals and undoubted piety should have control of the life both of soul and body, and they should be men and women with living wives and husbands. It should be the duty of the general superintendent to visit, not weekly but daily and hourly, every ward in the building, and power should be given him to fine every wardmaster or mistress for every oath he or she may be heard to swear, until they reach the amount of their wages, which is twenty dollars per month, I believe. By this means the morals of the institution would soon improve. At each meal he should see that every patient who is able to go to the table is in his place, and not let some poor man or woman lie in his or her cell sick or asleep and go without food and medicine; also before any one eats a morsel he should ask the blessing of God upon the provisions provided for them. There should be a chaplain to minister to them in holy things, and to pray for the sick and the dying, to hold morning and evening prayers, and to preach to the patients at least twice every Lord's day. Not only should their bodies be attended to, but their souls also. They should not permit a man or woman to die without spiritual comfort and be buried like a hog. If any place on earth should have all the means of grace, the insane hospital is the place. I do say there should be great improvement in this direction, and the sooner the better. May the good citizens of the United States awake to the importance of this subject. Let a man or woman be placed there for six months and hear but three short sermons read during that time, and they will think as I do, if they have lived where they have been blessed with these means of grace. Please let the members of the next legislatures that may meet in these United States of America look well to this hint. With proper laws and appointments to the several institutions of this character, there may be a great saving of souls, of bodies, and of money.

It is amusing to hear the sayings and witness the doings of many of the patients. There was an elderly gentleman in the asylum by the name of Ramsey, from Chilton County, originally from Hall County, Georgia. Meet him when you would, he was going home the next day; his family was coming after him. He said he had a large flock of blooded sheep both of Cotswold and of Southdown. I wished to buy of him, but he would not sell to me at any price. I doubt whether he had any sheep at all. There was another strange character there, Dr. Neilson. He was a man of considerable wealth, owned a large plantation near Tuscaloosa, and had a lucrative practice. He had been a member of the Methodist Church in the city. His losses during the war had so affected him that he became somewhat demented. He thought the Bishops of the M. E. Church, South, were the sole cause of the war and of his misfortunes. He said he was going to sue them for damages, and that his claims against them were twenty-five millions of dollars. On every other subject he was rational and was well posted. He was a tall, fine-looking man. He told me an incident about John A. Murrel that occurred in Tennessee. Soon after his inauguration into his stealing clan, he was out on a thieving tour and came across a large flock of sheep, five hundred in number. Late in the evening he selected one hundred of the largest of them, separated them from the flock and drove them off, following after them. They made for home and got there about dusk. He called at the house of the owner of the sheep and wished to stay all night. The owner opened his gate and counted them in. During the night he sold them to his host as a lot of Cotswolds for five dollars each. He had to leave early the next morning, went and gathered up the other four hundred, drove them to another farmer, and sold them for one dollar each, making in all nine hundred dollars.

But thank God, I am at home among my family and friends. While I was in prison I had nothing to do but to read and pray, and it (while reading and praying) was the happiest portion of my life. I prayed to be resigned to the will of God, and that I might perfectly acquiesce in his will in all things, and I believe, as I am taught, that "the steps of the good man are ordered by the Lord"; that he "delighteth in his way," and "though he fall, he shall not utterly be cast down," for the Lord upholdeth him with his hand; that "all things work together for good to them that love God." I prayed for myself first, until I got my own case properly before God, then for my wife, children, and grandchildren—forty nine in all at this time, but then forty seven, mentioning them all by name; also for the preacher on our circuit, J. T. Morris, with his family, and every member of every church on Munford Circuit; the preacher, the Rev. L. F. Whitten and his wife, of Talladega Circuit, and every member thereon; Dr. West, the presiding elder of the district, with the stationed preacher of Talladega, and numerous other friends and acquaintances throughout the county. Among those I thus prayed for personally were Marcus Cruikshank, General Wm. B. McLellan, Mrs. James Stockdale, Mrs. J. Towery, and Mrs. J. Orr, with their families; and every one of these persons are dead and gone to eternity.

Marcus Cruikshank was the editor of the Talladega Reporter and Watch Tower. He was also representative of this district at one time in the Congress of the Confederate States, and was one of the purest spirits I have ever known. Though a lawyer, he would always advise his clients to compromise all litigated cases. He might have had as large practice as any man at his bar if he had done as most attorneys do, get up as much litigation as possible. I find it very profitable to pray personally for relatives and friends. Last spring, just before I left home, a gentleman was speaking to me of a minister, who he said was the most successful teacher in getting his pupils converted he ever knew. The secret, he said, was in praying personally for and with them. I thought it a good plan, and concluded to try it that night with my youngest son, who had grown up to be a good big boy without being converted. I always have my children read the Scriptures for me at prayers, also to read me to sleep when I retire to rest, and it does not take long to do it. I had called on Howard a night or two before to read for me as I was retiring. He said he had to work hard and rise early, and wanted to go to bed himself, and disobeyed my wishes. This night at prayers I mentioned Howard, that God would convert him and make him a good boy. As soon as we arose from our knees, he said, "Pa, do you want me to read for you tonight?" He read for me very cheerfully and pleasantly.

CHAPTER XV

I SETTLED in Alabama in the year 1834, this making the forty-ninth crop made on the same plantation. I settled at an Indian town called Chinnobee, on Cheahhah, a small stream that makes out of the last spurs of the Alleghany Mountains. Chinnobee town is where lived the celebrated Indian chief Chinnobee, who piloted General Jackson from Fort Strother, on the Coosa River, to the battle of Talladega. Chinnobee, with the Indians of a few other towns, was friendly during the Indian wars from 1812 to 1814. These, seeing the danger to which they were exposed, built a fort half a mile southwest from the public square of the city of Talladega, where they were fortified when the Lower Creeks, or Red Sticks, as they called themselves, found them while on their way from below to give battle to Captain Jackson, as they called the general, he being fortified at or near Brother's Ferry on Coosa River, in what is now called St. Clair County. Jackson, on hearing of the terrible massacre at Fort Mims, where about five hundred men, women, and children were fortified, had raised twenty-five hundred men in Tennessee—two thousand militia and five hundred cavalry. The first settlers of Alabama had located in that section, and on account of the depredations of the Indians had built this fort for the protection of their families. While most of the men were out watching their cattle, at noon, the gates of the fort being open and the inmates at dinner, the Indians stole a march on the fort and destroyed the life of every inhabitant with the exception of twelve or fifteen. This enraged the friends of the slain, who were mostly Tennesseans. Jackson received the appointment to raise a force and chastise the enemy. He had got into the Creek territory with his army, and quartered at Fort Strother, as it is known on the United States map, where he was waiting for supplies to be shipped from East Tennessee down the Tennessee River to Gunter's Landing, and thence to be hauled across to Fort Strother, on the Coosa, when he intended to move upon the enemy. He was thus waiting, when the hostiles, or Red Sticks, found Chinnobee and his forces fortified in Talladega. They were surrounded by a large force, and Chinnobee was informed by them, though he claimed to be neutral, that if he and his force did not march with them against Jackson they would massacre the last one of them. Of course Chinnobee had to use some strategy to save the lives of his people. He agreed to join the hostiles provided they would allow his people three days' time to beat their meal and prepare for war.

The Red Sticks wished to go into his fort. Chinnobee objected, saying they had no room for them and their horses and dogs. It was their custom to carry their dogs with them on all occasions. Though the fort was guarded with a strong picket force, Chinnobee and Jim Fife, a half-breed, and chief of Conchartee town on the Choccolocco, stole out after dark by throwing a bearskin over them and putting on bells. They went grunting and rooting along like so many hogs. The Indians then kept their hogs belled. They went through the picket-lines in this way, then mounted a pony each and laid whip for sixteen or eighteen miles to Fort Strother. My father's youngest brother, John Camp, was standing sentinel when they arrived and inquired for Captain Jackson. Fife understood the English language. My uncle pointed out his markee, and crept up near them and saw by the moonlight the smoke rising from their horses. They reached Fort Strother about eleven o'clock the same night. They talked very rapidly and my uncle thought it would be wise to gather up his horse. He belonged to the cavalry under command of General Coffee. They had no forage and their horses were hobbled in the cane near by. Jackson gave orders for the army to be ready to march in thirty minutes. There was a terrible running and stumbling over logs after the horses. The cavalry had to take the whole army across the Coosa, six or eight hundred yards wide, on horseback, each horseman with a behind rider. It took them until day to get the army across. Next night the army camped on the north bank of Cheahhah, in what is now Mrs. English's plantation near Mr. S. M. Jennison's, and seven miles from Talladega. Jackson lay that night on one of the mounds in Mrs. English's field. It is generally believed that he marched his army down the Jackson Trace, crossing Choccolocco at Jackson's Shoals, but it is an error. He perhaps returned that way with his wounded, and did afterward open this route or trace. A little after sunrise on the morning of the third day he attacked the enemy, taking them by surprise. They were eating and lounging around their campfires; had stripped themselves of their buckskin leggins and piled them between two saplings about three hundred yards beyond the fort, near where Colonel Hogan settled on the branch below the big spring in Talladega. They were badly whipped. A great many were killed and wounded and some prisoners were taken. The entire force would have been captured if Jackson's orders had been obeyed. One of the officers failed to close up a gap, which if done would have surrounded the whole army. The officer was cashiered. Bill Scott and his wife were among the prisoners. Ira, his son, was born in prison. Bill was a silversmith among the Indians after I came to this country. Jackson lost seventeen killed and a hundred wounded. He hauled his wounded on litters back to Fort Strother. General Coffee commanded the cavalry during the whole campaign. He was piloted by Jim Fife, who was a good interpreter. He interpreted for the land speculators while they were negotiating for the lands belonging to the Indians. He called it "making physic"; that is, he would talk for them if they would pay him to "make physic." Chinnobee acted so bravely in the battle and did so much for the benefit of the whites that Jackson presented him with a fine uniform and gave him the title of general. He also presented him with a rifle finely inlaid with silver, with the inscription, "Presented to General Chinnobee by General Andrew Jackson." I have seen the gun often. After the general's death it fell into the hands of his eldest son, Arbiahkiah Hola, who carried it with him to Arkansas, when they emigrated to the Indian Territory. General Chinnobee was quite eloquent and stood high as a public man. He went to Washington city once in the interest of the Creek tribe. Jackson was then the President, and sitting in the Capitol talking to some men about brave men. Some one had treated Chinnobee until he became drunk, and was leaning against a wall heaving from drunkenness, when Jackson pointed to him and said, "There stands the bravest man I have ever seen." About the 10th of February, 1835, the next week after the "cold

Saturday," which was the 7th of February, 1835, I had been to Mobile. In those days we had no railroads. I rode horseback to Wetumpka and took the first steamboat I had ever seen to Mobile. I attended an auction of a large cargo of goods there which had been damaged in transportation. On my way home on the night of the cold Saturday at nine o'clock I had just gone to my berth to lie down, when I heard the engineer ring the bell. I thought it was to land, and put my face to a glass door to see what place it was, when the boat came in collision with another boat called the Chippewah. It was going south, and the wind blew the smoke right in the direction of the Farmer, the boat I was on. The shock was dreadful. It knocked over stoves and cut heads badly. The Chippewah had on her bow a statue of the Chippewah chief. The next morning we had him aboard our vessel. Almost all the guards of our boat were gone. We landed in Wetumpka during the night. There I found some of my neighbors and we came home together on horseback. In passing Mardisville, five miles below Talladega town, we found General Chinnobee and Jim Fife. Mardisville was where the land-office was located for the Coosa Land District. Chinnobee discovered me riding along the street and came to me and told me he wished to go home with me. I discovered he was drinking and told him I had company and that he could overtake me. I rode on and he and Fife got their horses. Chinnobee was riding a fine race-horse belonging to his son. They put out on their horses at full speed. About a quarter of a mile above Mardisville there was a large post-oak standing in the middle of the road. The road ran on both sides of the tree. It seemed the horse was aiming for one side and Chinnobee for the other. Chinnobee was dashed against the tree and his skull broken. Fife overtook me and told me Chinnobee was dead. The citizens of Mardisville purchased a shroud and fine coffin and wished to bury him with the honors of war, but his family objected and brought him home and buried him in his own dwelling. They always bury their dead in their houses. His remains now lie on Cheahhah, nine miles northeast of Talladega, on Colonel Thomas McEldeny's place, within two hundred yards of his residence.

General Chinnobee lived about twenty-two years after the war. He was opposed to leaving his country, as were many others of the tribe. I went with Mr. Wheat, who had contracted with the government to remove the Indians west of the Mississippi River, to see Chinnobee and learn whether he would be willing to move. Mr. Wheat urged the advantages he would derive from emigrating west. He said he would not do so, that he was too old and feeble.

The contractor told him he would have wagons for him, to which he replied that he went to Washington city once in a wagon and it turned over with him and broke his leg, and he would ride no more in wagons. He had gone there once in a stage-coach, for that was the only way of travel before the time of railroads, and the stage turned over and broke his leg, and he was opposed to traveling in wagons. I doubt if he had lived his ever going to the territory.

Colonel Thomas McEldeny was with General Coffee, who commanded the cavalry at the decisive battle of the Horse-Shoe, on the Tallapoosa River, where Bill Rutherford was so badly whipped by Jackson that he never tried to give battle again. The Indian fortification was in a bend of the river, the bend resembling a horse-shoe, which gave it the name. The river made a bend including several hundred acres, and ran back to within a few hundred yards of the river again, and across this neck of land the Indians had strong breastworks. Jackson, in trying to reach this stronghold, before the battle spoken of, was surprised at a late hour of the night, four miles from the Horse-shoe at a place called Emuckfaw, and was whipped, if Rutherford had known it. Rutherford was in command of the Creeks, and was as brave as Julius Caesar. Jackson was so badly whipped that he turned back the next day with his forces, and while crossing the Nitiechopco was ambushed and came near losing his whole army. He lost one of his cannon, but went on to Fort Williams, situated on the Coosa River in the southwestern part of Talladega County, where he recruited his forces and then made his successful campaign to the destruction of the Creek tribe. After obtaining recruits, Jackson moved on to the Horse-shoe. The fortification was on the north side of the river. He sent his cavalry below to a point that was fordable, with instructions to surround the bend, and when in position to give the sign by blowing a horn or bugle. He marched with the main army to a little pine hill in front of the breast-works, planted his cannon, and opened fire, and thus continued firing while General Coffee was getting his men in position. At first he topped the trees with grapeshot. The Indians said he was drunk and was shooting his wagons at them. From where the cavalry was stationed across the river, Colonel Thomas McEldeny told me, the smoke of the cannon could be seen a considerable time before the report was heard. General Coffee with his men swam the river and took the canoes that lined the banks of the north side, where the enemy was located, and set fire to their buildings, while Jackson attracted them with his army and big guns and hewing down the timber with balls. The order was given to storm the works. An old Irishman by the name of Matson, from East Tennessee, father of William Matson, now of Talladega County, was among the first to scale the wall. He threw down his gun and said, "Be jabbers, and heare ye are, and be jabbers, heare is Johnnie Matson!" and pitched into them fist and skull. Sam Houston was also among the first to scale the breast-works, but while climbing over an Indian arrow pierced his thigh. The arrow was barbed and he could not extract it. He called on a comrade to pull it out. He replied he could not. Houston told him if he did not do so he would kill him. The man wrenched it out and Houston was sent back among the wounded, but in a few minutes had his thigh bound up with a handkerchief and was again in the midst of the fight. Houston was a poor boy. Soon after he was wounded he said his fortune was made, and sure enough it was. It was he who whipped Santa Anna, the great Mexican general, at San Jacinto and gained Texas. He was made governor of the Lone Star State, and was as much honored by the Texans as General Washington was by the people of the colonies.

Chapter XVI

A BROTHER of Gen'l Chinnobee by the name of Coffee (they were called by a White and an Indian name), with Andy Lundie, Charlie, and several other Indians, after they had agreed to emigrate, and had been taken one hundred miles from their homes to Wetumpka to be shipped by steamboat, were camped with a large number of wagoners on the bank of the Coosa. They told the poor Indians that when the steamboat came they intended to tie them and put them aboard like so many hogs. On the arrival of the boat they broke like wild steers and took to the hills. Coffee and his party did not see a white man nor were they seen by one until they reached Chinnobee town, and came into Joseph Coker's (my half brother) very nearly starved. They had had nothing to eat from the time they left Wetumpka. Coker gave them something to eat. Coffee and his party settled at the head of Cheahhah, which means Potato Creek. At an early day after the whites settled this country we established a camp-ground in Chinnobee town, near Joseph Coker's, a point which was well watered, and it was called Chinnobee Camp-ground. Hundreds were converted there. Among the tenters were Rev. James Stockdale, Rev. J. L. Seay, Rev. J. B. Seay, Jesse Fain, Judge J. E. Groce, Alex Porter, Massingale Porter, Jesse Matson, William Matson, G. W. Penn, William Carpenter, Rev. Alex Douglass, and Eli Cowser, with myself. In those days we had in the local ranks of Methodist preachers men that were Boanerges, such as Revs. Leonard Tarrant, Harris Taylor, Edward Patton, James Stockdale, John Brooks, Hardin, and Nicholas P. Scales, William McLelland, John L. Seay, Benjamin Stripling, J. B. Seay, William Rideout, Sylvanus Swope, Hendrick, and others. Those old-time meetings were among the most glorious I have ever witnessed. Hundreds were converted, many of whom became preachers. Among them were Dr. Joseph Scales, Neil Brown, Robert Ragan, and others who went to Texas. Though the local preachers have no voice in the Annual or General Conference, they have done as much as or more to establish Methodism in this country than the regular itinerant. Very much of the establishing of the church in Talladega County is due to the zeal of Judge Leonard Tarrant. Though in public life, he would never let that prevent his holding two-days' meetings all over this country. I have known him after he was three score and ten to leave Mardisville on Saturday morning and ride from fifteen to twenty miles before eleven o'clock to hold a two-days' meeting.

One Sunday night, during a camp-meeting held at Chinnobee, after there had been quite a revival at the altar, where many professed religion, we had left the arbor and gone to our tents. The negroes gathered at the stand to worship. Old Coffee and all the rest of the Indians that did not emigrate worshiped with the colored people. A negro man belonging to Bro. Seay was a local preacher, and it was said he could beat his master preaching, and that was hard to do, for J. L. Seay is one of the greatest natural men I have ever known. Henry had preached and invited penitents to the altar. I heard a beautiful song. The negroes could beat the whites singing. The song was new to me and I lay on ray bed and listened. It was so full of melody I arose and sat in the tent-door and thought to try to learn it. Finally, I went down to the stand, and there was Coffee prostrate on his knees in the altar, with an altar full of penitents. The old Indian was weeping as though his heart would break and smiting his breast saying, "Enokequa sulga"—my heart is sick. I never had such sympathy for any one in life. To think that his people were all in the West and he with his wife and few others left behind, cut off from his associates, and he weeping so bitterly. I encouraged and instructed him as best I could, but he did not understand English. At last he obtained the blessing and cried out, "Enokequa sosagus"—sickness all gone. He arose clapping his hands, with tears streaming from his eyes and a beaming countenance, and praising God. Next morning he with about one hundred other converts gave his hand to Judge Tarrant to join the church. Bro. Tarrant insisted as many as were heads of families should take up the cross and establish the family altar, at the same time saying, "We are anxious to feed our bodies three times a day, and we should be equally anxious to feed the soul; that it is as much impossible to enjoy the life and power of

religion without prayer as it is for the body to exist without food." Coffee
went home and took up family prayer, and for several years and so long as he
lived in this country he prayed in his family three times a day.

Knowing that we need provision for the body at least three times a day,
I do believe that we should hold family worship as often. One of the most
religious men I have known was the Rev. E. J. Hamill, whose universal
practice was to pray seven times a day besides his public ministrations. The
Psalmist teaches, in the 119th Psalm, 164th verse, "Seven times a day do
I praise thee, because of thy righteous judgments." I think at morning we
should

> Wash our face and comb our hair,
> Kneel down and say our prayer;

also to pray with our family, and three times a day, or as often as we eat,
should retire to the closet and pray in secret. Should pray with our family
every evening, and when we retire to rest should commit the keeping of
our soul and body to our Father in heaven; which makes seven times a
day. The Psalmist did so, and we have the same need as he.

> The happiest men I ever saw
> Were those who prayed the most;
> Their souls were full of Jesus
> And the Holy Ghost.

A few days since I visited that good old brother, Judge J. E. Groce. He is
perfectly blind. As soon as we finished eating dinner he asked me to lead
him to his parlor, and said, "Let us kneel and pray in secret." This is his daily
custom, and though he is blind is perfectly resigned to his affliction and
happy all the time. He says God is good to him, for "whomsoever he loveth
he chasteneth."

But I must say something more about Judge Tarrant. He was certainly
one among the best of men. He was appointed the certifying agent of the
Creek Indians by Andrew Jackson, while President of the United States,
and I doubt whether he could have made a better selection in the United
States. His business was to see that the Indians were not defrauded out
of their lands. There were two land-offices established, the Coosa and the
Tallapoosa. The Judge's district was the Coosa. It seemed the government
did all it could to protect the Indian rights. Before their land could be

purchased, the purchaser had to have it valued by two disinterested men. They had to make affidavit that it was worth so much and no more, and the purchaser had to give this amount and as much more as the Indian asked before the contract could or would be certified by the agent. At least this was the law. After the Indians had traded away their country, they reserved for themselves one half-section to each head of a family and to their chiefs, one whole section. The country was surveyed, and the oldest settler on the land took his reservation under him. The others were floated by an agent and located on the best lands in the country. The name of each owner, with the number of his land, was furnished to the judge. Soon after, speculators got in and purchased all they could get. The country was full of land-buyers. Some of the Indians would not sell. A company of land-stealers formed about Columbus, Georgia, and gathered up Indians who had sold their lands and spent the money for whisky, and would get them to assume the names of other Indians who had not sold, take them to the land-office with their men, who would value their land. It could not be supposed that the agent would know all the Indians. In one week I understood there were five hundred fraudulent contracts made in Tallapoosa District. The company came up to Mardisville and told Judge Tarrant if he would resign his appointment and let another agent be appointed in his stead, that they would make him an equal partner and besides would give him twenty-five thousand dollars. This offer was made late one evening. The judge, not suspecting their object, said it was a very great temptation to him, and told them he would consider the matter. He told me that he prayed over it nearly all night. He went to his office early the next morning, when he promised to give them an answer. He said, "Gentlemen, you can not bribe me." They were taken with a leaving. Some men were in Washington talking to Andrew Jackson about the Alabamians, and said they did not believe there was an honest man in Alabama. Jackson replied, "It is not so; Leonard Tarrant is there." The judge was in moderate circumstances, and could and would have accepted the offer if he had not been an honest man. He believed "honesty the best policy." He died triumphantly several years since. I saw him upon his death-bed. He spoke of death with as much calmness as if he were going to take a journey. He has gone, and "his works do follow him." "Let me die the death of the righteous."

This land-stealing was the cause of the last Creek war. The President was informed of the land-frauds, and he sent to this country a company of investigating agents, to investigate the fraudulent contracts. To prevent investigation, the land-company persuaded the lower Creeks to get up the war with the Indians in 1836. Notwithstanding, the agents came, and out of all the contracts made in Judge Tarrant's district but about one was found which was not valid. It was the Tallapoosa District in which so much corruption existed. There might be volumes written about the history of this country.

Chapter XVII

*F*OR the benefit of some into whose hands this book may fall, I do not think it amiss to relate some gleanings of history during and since my stay at the hospital.

The first white man who was ever on the soil of Alabama was De Soto. On Sunday the 18th of November, 1540, after remaining at Manvilla eight days, De Soto issued his orders for his troops to take up the march in a northwardly direction, which order fell upon the entire force like a clap of thunder, for it was generally expected when the march was commenced Maldinado's ship at Ochus was the anticipated point of march. The order, however, was obeyed and the line of march taken up, which proceeded northwardly through the present Clarke County where Grove Hill and Mott's Post Office are now situated, and through a most fertile and productive country called Pafallaya, and thickly dotted with Indian villages, entering the present county of Marengo about where Dixon's Mills are located, and a few miles farther on a large and populous town was reached called in the Indian dialect Talepotana, where De Soto and his troops encamped five days. The march was then renewed, and the route was through the now Marengo County, where Linden and Spring Hill are now located, and entering the present county of Hale near the present Macon station, on the Alabama Central Railroad, reaching the Warrior River about six miles below the site of old Erie, where a large Indian city was found, called by the savages Cabusta, the inhabitants of which were intensely hostile, offering battle to the Spaniards in vast numbers from both sides of the river. Thousands of savages lined the opposite side of the river for miles, making every hostile demonstration possible. A force of some two thousand savages attacked the Spanish force and were successfully repulsed, those not killed or wounded swimming the river to join those on the west side of the river. De Soto then moved his forces up to Cabusta, where the present town of Erie is located, in Hale County, the inmates of all classes, sizes, and kinds fleeing to the woods on his approach. Here the Spaniards were attacked every night by the savages, who crossed the river from the opposite side in canoes. So annoying were these attacks that De Soto had impassable ditches cut between his camp and the river-bluff, in which troops were stationed armed with cross-bows and arquebuses. This precaution caused the night attacks to cease; but the attacks were renewed in the day by the savages attempting to cross the river in fleets of canoes, resulting each time in a complete annihilation of the savages, the limpid waters of the Warrior becoming tinged with red by savage blood.

De Soto had constructed in the woods near by two large flat-boats, which were hauled by horses to the river several miles above and launched during the night. In these boats cavalry and infantry were placed, and swiftly moved across the river. The first were literally covered with showers of arrows; but the river being low and narrow troops were crossed rapidly, and soon De Soto with eighty men reached the opposite side, who leading about two hundred men of his forces, attacked the savages, who had assembled a large force and showered arrows upon the Spaniards, who hewed them down like blades of grass, until only a few could escape to the woods. In a few hours the entire Spanish force had crossed the river, the savages in the meantime centering their entire force at a point about one mile from the river, which they had strongly fortified by palisades, and from which the savages would make raids upon the Spaniards all the day. Next morning De Soto led his entire force against this fortified point, and after a short resistance the fortification was entered by the Spaniards and a most terrible slaughter of the savages ensued, male and female young and old engaging in the conflict. No distinction was made by the infuriated Spaniards; but slaughtering all that made resistance to their swords and battle-axes. The result of this conflict was a complete destruction of that tribe of savages. De Soto continued his march in a northwest direction from Cabusta, through the present Green County, and passing through Daniel Prairie, Clinton, Pleasant Ridge, thence into Pickens County by Bridgeville, reaching the little Bigbee River at the now Ringo's Bluff, and thence up the river to the point now occupied by Pickensville, where the forces crossed the little Bigbee River, and went out of the Alabama Territory December 14, 1540, and entered the Mississippi Territory about where the present village of Grantville is, making the march from Manvilla, upon the Alabama, to the Mississippi State-line in twenty-six days, making the occupation of Alabama by this distinguished warrior,

from the 9th of July, 1540, to the 14th of December of the same year, five
months and five days.

It is not within our purpose to continue the interesting journal of De
Soto, the brave discoverer of Alabama, or to relate the thrilling incidents
after leaving Alabama soil, and his sad end, by his remains being buried
in the Mississippi River in a coffin made by hewing out a poplar tree. But
in concluding an account of this famous man's career on Alabama soil we
can say that the history of his life, as given especially by Garcilasso de la
Vega, is one of the most thrilling histories of man, and unequalled by that
of Napoleon Bonaparte.

CHAPTER XVIII

*A*BOUT the year 1777 many persons of the then colonies, fearful of the consequences of the war then commencing for the independence of the colonies, removed and sought a home beyond their limits. Some selected the Tombigbee and others the Mississippi rivers, and braving the horrors of the wilderness, made a home for themselves and posterity amid the rude inhospitalities of uncultivated nature. There were at that time small settlements of French and Spanish adventurers upon these streams, in different localities.

La Salle descended from Canada, and taking possession of Louisiana, it created among many of the chivalrous and adventurous spirits of France a desire to take possession of the entire country from the mouth of the St. Lawrence River to the mouth of the Mississippi. Nova Scotia, called Acadia by its first settlers, and the provinces of Canada, were his already, and France desired to restrict the further expansion of the English colonies, now growing to importance along the Atlantic coast. The vast extent of the continent and its immense fertility, with its mighty rivers, its peculiar adaptation to settlement, and the yielding of all the necessaries and luxuries of human wants, had aroused the enterprise of Europe. Spain had possessed herself of South America, Mexico, and Cuba, the pride of the Antilles. The success of her scheme of colonization stimulated both England and France to push forward the settlements and to foster and protect them from governmental care. After some fruitless attempts the mouth of the Mississippi had been discovered and approached from the Gulf. The expedition under La Salle had failed to find it. The small colony brought by him for settlement upon the Mississippi had been landed many leagues west of the river's mouth, and owing to the disputes between that great and enterprising man and the officers commanding the two ships which had transported them across the Atlantic, they were mercilessly left by this officer without protection and almost without provision on the coast of what is now Texas. La Salle had started with a small escort by land to find the great river. These men became dissatisfied; and not sharing in the adventurous and energetic spirit of their leader, remonstrated with him and proposed to return to his companions, but disregarding them, he pressed on in his new enterprise. In wading a small stream, one of the men was carried off by an alligator, and in a day or so after another was bitten by a rattlesnake. Terror seized upon his men, and all their persuasions proving fruitless, they determined to assassinate him and return. They did so, only to find the colony dispersed and nowhere to be found. After many hazardous adventures they reached the Arkansas River and descended it to its mouth, where they proposed preparing some means of ascending the Mississippi and thus return to Canada. Fortunately they had been there but a few hours when a small boat or two, which had been dispatched from Canada to look after the colony so long expected, arrived, and learning the unfortunate issue of the enterprise, took on board the party and returned up the river. They reported the colony destroyed, and it was not until many years after that it was discovered that those left on the seaside had been found and conveyed to the Jesuit Mission at San Antonio, where they had been cared for, and preserved by the pious and humane missionaries. Subsequently a colony was located at Biloxi, on the shore of the lake, and thence was transferred to New Orleans. Mobile was soon after made the nucleus of another colony, and from these two points had proceeded the pioneers of the different settlements along these rivers — the Tombigbee and the Mississippi. It was to these settlements that the refugees from the revolutionary in the colonies had retired. Natchez and St. Francisville, on the Mississippi, and St. Stephens and McIntosh Bluff, on the Tombigbee, were the most populous and important. About these, and under the auspicious protection of the Spanish government, then dominant in Louisiana and Florida, commenced the growth of the Anglo-Norman population, which is now almost the entire population of the country.

There proceeded from South Carolina, about the time mentioned above, a colony of persons which located near Natchez. They came down the Holston, Tennessee, and Mississippi rivers on flatboats, and after many escapes from the perils incident to the streams they navigated and the hostility of the savages who dwelt along the shores, they reached the Canaan of their hopes. They had intended to locate at New Madrid. The country around was well suited for cultivation, being alluvial and rich, and the climate was all they could desire; but they found a population mongrel and vicious, unrestrained by law or morals, and learning through a negro belonging to the place of an intended attack upon their party for the purpose of robbery, they hastily reembarked what of their property and their stock they had debarked, under pretense of dropping a few miles down the river for a more eligible site. They silently and secretly left in the night and never attempted another stop until reaching the Walnut Hills, now Vicksburg. A few of the party concluded to remain here while the larger number went on down, some to the mouth of Coles's Creek, some to Natchez, and others to the Cliffs known by the name of one of the emigrants whose party concluded to settle there.

These cliffs, which are eighteen miles below Natchez, have always been known as Ellis's Cliffs. In their rear is a most beautiful and eminently fertile county. Grants were obtained from the Spanish government of these lands in tracts suited to the means of each family. A portion was given to the husband, a portion to the wife, and a portion to each child of every family. These grants covered nearly all that desirable region south of St. Catherine's Creek and west of the second creek to the Mississippi River and south to the Homochitto River. Similar grants were obtained for lands about the mouth and along the banks of Coles's Creek at and around Fort Adams, ten miles below the mouth of Red River and upon the Bayou Pierre. The same authority donated to the emigrants lands along the McIntosh Bluff, Fort St. Stevens, and along Bassett's Creek, in the region of the Tombigbee River. Here the lands were not so fertile nor in such bodies as in the region of the Mississippi. The settlements did not increase and extend to the surrounding country with the same rapidity that they increased in the latter country.

Many of those first stopping on the Tombigbee ultimately removed to the Mississippi. Here they encountered none of the perils or losses incident to the revolution. The privations of a new country they did of necessity endure, but not to the same extent that those suffer who are deprived of a market for the products of their labor. New Orleans afforded a remunerative market for all they could produce, and in return supplied them with every necessary beyond their means of producing at home. The soil and climate were not only auspicious to the production of cotton, tobacco, and indigo (then a valuable marketable commodity), but every facility for rearing without stint, every variety of stock. These settlements were greatly increased by emigration from Pennsylvania, subsequently to the conclusion of the war, as well as from the Southern States.

Very many who in the war had sided with the mother country from conscientious or mercenary views, were compelled by public opinion or by the operation of the law confiscating their property and banishing them from the country to find new homes. Those, however, who came first had choice of locations and most generally selected the best, and bringing most wealth maintained the ascendency in this regard and gave tone and direction to public matters as well as to the social organizations of society. Most of them were men of education and high social position in the countries from which they came. Constant intercourse with New Orleans and the education of the youth of both sexes of this region in the schools of that city carried the high polish of French society into the colony.

Louisiana, and especially New Orleans, was first settled by the nobility and gentry of France. They were men in position among the first of that great and glorious people. Animated with the ambition for high enterprise, they came in sufficient numbers to create a society and to plant French manners and customs and the elegance of French learning and French society upon the banks of Mississippi. The commercial and social intermingling of these people resulted in intermarriages, which very soon assimilated them in most things as one people, at least in feeling, sentiment, and interest. From such a stock grew the people inhabiting the banks of the Mississippi from Vicksburg to New Orleans. In 1826 young men of talent and enterprise had come from Europe and every section of the United States, and giving their talents to the development of the country, had created a wealth greater and more generally diffused than was at that time to be found in any other planting or farming community in the United States. Living almost exclusively among themselves, their manners and feelings were homogeneous, and living, too, almost entirely upon the products of their plantations, independent of their market-crops, they grew rich so rapidly as to mock the fable of Jonah's gourd. This wealth afforded the means of education and travel; these, cultivation and high mental attainments; and with these, the elegancies of refined life. The country was vast and fertile. The Mississippi flowing by their homes was sublimely grand, and seemed to inspire ideas and inspirations commensurate with its own majesty in the people upon its borders. In no country are to be found women of more refined character, more beauty, or more elegance of manners than among the planters wives and daughters of the Mississippi coast. Reared in the country, and accustomed to exercise in the open air, in walking through the shady avenues of the extensive and beautifully ornamented grounds about the home or plantation house, riding on horseback along the river's margin, elevated upon the levy covered with green Bermuda grass smoothly spreading over all the ground, save the pretty open road stretching through this grass like a thread of silver in a cloth of green, with the great drab river moving in silent majesty on one side, and the extensive fields of the plantation, teeming with the crop of cane or cotton upon the other. Their exercise, thus surrounded, becomes a school, and their ideas expand and grow with the sublimity of their surroundings. Here in these palatial homes was the hospitality of princes. It was not the hospitality of pride or ostentation, but of the heart, the welcome which the soul ungrudgingly gives and which delights and refines the receiver. It is the welcome of a refined humanity, untainted with selfishness and felt as a humane and duty-bound tribute to civilization and Christianity; such hospitality as can only belong to the social organization which had been obtained in the community from its advent upon this great country.

The independence of the planters' pursuit, the institution of domestic slavery, and the form and spirit of the government, all conduce to this. The mind is untrammeled and the soul is independent because subservient neither to the tyrannical exactions of unscrupulous authority or the more debasing servility of dependence upon the capricious whims of petty officials or a moneyed aristocracy. Independently possessing the soil and the labor for its cultivation, with only the care necessary to the comforts and necessities of this labor, superadded to those of a family, they were without the necessity of soliciting or courting favors from any one, or of pandering to the ignorant caprices of a labor beyond their control. Independence of means is the surest guarantee of independence of character. Where this is found, most private and most public virtues accompany it. Truth, sincerity, and all cardinal virtues are fostered most where there is most independence. This takes away the source of all corruption, all temptation. This seeks dependence and victimizes its creatures to every purpose of corruption and meanness. Under the influences of the institutions of the South, as they were, there was little of the servile meanness so predominant where they were not, and the lofty, chivalrous character of the southern people grew out of them.

Chapter xix

The Slave, His Adaptation to the Southern Climate and for Labor — His Mental and Moral Capacity — The Progress of Wealth and Science During the Two Hundred Years of American Slavery

*T*HE slave was a class below all others. His master was his protector and friend. He supplied his wants, he redressed his wrongs, and it was a point of honor as well as duty to do so. He was assured of his care and protection and felt no humility at his condition. The white man without means was reminded that, though poor, he was above the slave, and was stimulated with the pride of position as contrasted with that of the slave. His political, legal, and social rights were unrestrained and equal with those of the wealthiest. This was the only distinction between him and the wealthiest of the land, and this wealth conferred no exclusive privilege and its acquisition was open to his energy and enterprise, and he gloried in his independence. He could acquire and enjoy without dependence, and his pride and ambition were alike stimulated to the emulation of those who shared most fortune's favors.

The product of slave-labor, when directed by a higher intelligence than his own, is enormous, and was the basis of the extended and wealth-creating commerce of the entire country. These products could be obtained in no other manner, and without this labor, are lost to the world. The African negro, in osseous and muscular developments and in all the essentials for labor, is quite equal to the white race; in his cerebral, he is greatly inferior. The capacities of his brain are limited and incapable of cultivation beyond a certain point. His moral man is as feeble and unteachable as his mental. He can not be educated to the capacity of self-government nor to formation and conducting of civil government, to the extent of humanizing and controlling by salutary laws a people aggregated into communities. He learns by example, which he imitates so long as the example is before him, but this imitation never hardens to fixed views or habits, indicating the design of Providence, that their physical capacities should be directed and appropriated for good by an intelligence beyond the mental reach of the negro. Why is this so? In the wisdom and economy of creation, every created thing represents a design for use. The soil and climate of the tropical and semitropical regions of the earth produce and mature all or very nearly all the necessaries and luxuries of human life. But human beings of different races and different capacities fill up the whole earth. The capacity to build a fire and fabricate clothing is given only to man. Was the element of fire and the material for clothing given for any but man's use? This enables him to inhabit every clime. But the capacity to produce all the necessaries and luxuries of life is given only to a certain portion of the earth's surface, and its peculiar motions give the fructifying influence of the sun only to the middle belt of the planet. The use of this organization is evidenced in the productions of this belt, and these productions must be the result of intelligently directed labor. The peculiarity of the physical organization of the white man makes it impossible for him to labor both healthfully and efficiently for the greatest development of this favored region. Yet his wants demand the yield and tribute of this region. His inventive capacity evolved sugar from the wild canes of the tropics, than which nothing is more essential to his necessities save the cereals and clothing. He fabricated clothing from the tropical grass and tropical cotton, found the uses of cassia pimento, the dye-woods, and a thousand other tropical products which contribute to comfort, to necessity, and luxury, advancing human happiness, human progress, and human civilization.

The black man's organization is radically different. He was formed especially to live and labor in these tropical and semitropical regions of the earth. But he is naturally indolent; his wants are few and nature unaided supplies them. He is uninventive and has always from creation down lived among these plants without the genius to discover or the skill and industry to develop their uses. That they are used and that they contribute to human health and human necessities, is abundant evidence of Divine design in their creation. The black man's labor, then, and the white man's intelligence are necessary to the production and fabrication for human use of these provisions of Providence. This labor the black man will not yield without compulsion. He is eminently useful under this compulsion and useless even to himself without it. That he was designed to obey this authority and to be most happy when and where he was most useful, is apparent in his mental and moral organization. By moral, I mean those functions of the nervous system which bring us in relation to the external world. He aspires to nothing but the gratification of his passions and the indulgence of his indolence. He feels the oppression of slavery only when compelled to work, and none of the moral degradation incident to servility in the higher or superior races. He is consequently more happy and better contented in this than any other condition in life. In the two hundred years of African slavery, the world's progress was greater in the arts and sciences and in all the appliances promotive of intelligence and human happiness than in any other period of historical time of five centuries. Why? Because the labor was performed by the man formed for labor and incapable of thinking, and releasing the man formed to think, direct, and invent from labor other than the labor of thought. This influence was felt over the civilized world. The productions of the tropics were demanded by the higher civilization. Men forgot to clothe themselves in skins when they could do so in cloth. As Camera extended her flight, bearing these rich creations of labor elaborated by intelligence, civilization went with her, expanding the mind, enlarging the wants, and prompting progress in all with whom she communicated. Its influence was first felt from Antilles, extending to the United States. In proportion to the increase of these products was the increase of commerce, wealth, intelligence, and power. Compare the statistics of production by slave-labor with the increase of commerce, and they go hand in hand. As the slave came down from the grain-growing region to the cotton- and sugar-region, the amount of his labor's product entering into commerce increased fourfold. The inventions of Whitney and Arkwright cheapened the fabric of cotton so much as to bring it within the reach of the poorest and availed the world in all the uses of cloth. The shipping and manufacturing interest of England grew. Those of the United States, from nothing, in a few years were great rivals of the mother country, and very soon surpassed her in commercial tonnage. Every interest prospered with the prosperity of the planter of the Southern States. His class has passed away. The weeds blacken where the chaste white cotton beautified his fields. His slave is a freedman, a constitution-maker, a ruler set up by a fanaticism to control his master and to degrade and destroy his country. This must bear its legitimate fruit. It is the beginning of the end of the negro upon this continent. Two races with the same civil, political, and social privileges can not long exist in harmony together. The struggle for supremacy will come, and with it a war of races. Then God have mercy on the weaker. The mild compulsion which stimulated his labor is withdrawn, and with it the care and protection which alone preserved him. He works no more. His day of jubilee has come. He must be a power in the land. Infatuated creature! You can not see or calculate the inevitable destiny now fixed for your race. You can not see the vile uses you are made to subserve for a time; or deem that those who now appear your conservators are but preparing your funeral-pyre.

Chapter xx

*T*HE plain republican habits which characterized the people of upper
Georgia and Alabama in her early settlements and growth, together with the
fact of the very moderate means of the people, exercised a powerful influence
in the formation of the character of her people. They had no large commercial
city, and her commerce was confined to the simple disposal of the surplus
products of her soil and the supply of the few wants of the people. It was
a cardinal virtue to provide every thing possible of the absolute necessaries
of life at home. The provision crop was of first necessity and secured the
first attention of the farmer. The market crop was ever secondary and was
only looked to to supply those necessaries which could not be grown upon
the plantation. These were salt, iron, and steel first; then if there remained
unexhausted some of the proceeds of the crop, a small, always a small, supply
of sugar and coffee, and for rare occasions a little tea. Tea for general use was
made of sassafras-roots, which I think the best of all the teas and far more
healthy. If it cost seventy-five cents or one dollar a pound it would be used in
preference. The coffee which in those early times cost fifty cents per pound
was used very sparingly, could not be afforded more than once or twice a
week by the wealthiest families. I remember well when there was no cotton
raised in any of the States for market. Tobacco was the staple commodity,
and that had to be rolled in hogsheads. My father had to carry his tobacco
to Augusta, one hundred and ten miles distant, which was the nearest
market. They tied the tobacco, just stripped from the stalk, in hands, which
they put into small bundles or hands, as we do fodder, and pressed into
hogsheads, and made to weigh fifteen hundred or two thousand pounds.

With gudgeons in the center of each head, they would attach shalves or tongue, and would also put felloes around each end, so as to raise the bulge or middle of the hogshead off the ground, and by hitching from one to three horses, according to size, would roll them to market. Sometimes the hoops would come loose and perhaps be nailed at one end. Every time the barrel would turn over, the end of the hoop would slap the horse and cause him to run. My father came near being run over by a runaway horse caused by a hoop coming loose at one end. The faster the horse ran, the more he was whipped. The little cotton that was raised was picked from the seed by the family with their fingers. Up to this time we raised flax, of which was made all or nearly all our wearing-apparel. Most of the first settlers wore buckskin pants. Once during the revolutionary war there came a squad of Tories to my grandfather's house and robbed him of all his wearing-apparel. About the time they had collected all the clothing together they discovered my grandfather had on a very fine pair of new buckskin pants, which had been made with silk thread. They ordered him to give them to them. He refused and ran to his gun-rack, and gathered his gun. The Tories cocked their guns and pointed at him. His only daughter, a little girl ten years old, seeing his danger ran to him and tore them off, screaming as she did so as if she would go into spasms. He was left in his nether garment and but for his little daughter, Winnifred, would have been killed.

I was ten years old before I ever saw a common road-wagon. The vehicles used were made of what we call truck-wheels, made by sawing off gum-logs. The sled or truck-wagon was the only wagon used seventy years ago.

The people were not so fastidious then as now. The young ladies, also the old, would walk four and five miles to church, would wear their old shoes or go barefoot to near the church, then put on their shoes and hide their old ones behind a log until they would return from church. People in those early days had to economize.

I did take my anticipated trip to Georgia in December last and visited our old homestead. It is astonishing how every thing will diminish in magnitude. Hills and mountains, houses and farms, water-courses and distances diminish in magnitude about fifty per cent. I went into the house where I was born and raised, also to the spring where in my boyhood father had built a stone spring-house and pitched the roof with tar; but the spring-house had fallen down.

Just here I beg my kind reader to bear with me in the narration of events of the sweet long ago. Although the place where I was born and the place where I have lived and reared my family are not exceeding two or three hundred miles apart, my life has been so absorbed in the rearing of my family, the cultivation and improvement of my farm, and the general interests of the country in which I live, that these scenes of the olden time have been buried with the past, until now I seem to live over again boyhood's happy-hours, and my soul is stirred within me. I had visited the old home some thirty years since in company with my Brother Benjamin. Neither of us had seen the place for twenty years. It was in the month of June. Some relatives were with us—Uncle David Thompson, Bro. Hope, and old Father Whaley. They lived in the immediate neighborhood, took no interest in the place, and rode on to a house near by. After looking at the old springhouse and finding the shingle roof father had put on rotted off, and a clapboard roof then on, I went in the direction of an old barn, then standing in the horse-lot, where in childhood I held my secret prayers. I went in, fell down on my knees, and thanked God for his preserving care, and felt very humble. We went back to the house. The family, whom I knew, was out. The doors were open, and I told my brother I wished to go into the room where I was born. We went in, knelt down together, and returned thanks to God for his merciful Providence in sparing us through so many dangers seen and unseen. If the family had come in and found us they would have supposed us a couple of lunatics escaped from some asylum. We also visited a mill that was built by my father in the year 1800. He blew off a rock that jutted over a fine freestone spring, and while dressing his mill-rocks pecked the initials of his name and the date thereon—" J. C. 1800." It is there today, as plain as when he put it there eighty-two years ago. The house in which I was born was built in the year 1799. I had supposed it a very large building, but it is quite a small affair. I visited also the old widowed aunts mentioned in the beginning of my narrative. One of them, Drucilla Thompson, is ninety years old and lives in the house built by my grandfather, Thomas Camp, in 1799. It is a log building, ceiled and weather boarded and pitched with tar, and is perfectly sound yet. Tar seems to preserve wood better than paint. The other aunt, Nancy Smith, is eighty-eight years of age, is quite lively and cheerful. I tried to preach there at old Bethlehem third Sabbath in December last. It was first known, when I was a child, as Atkins's Meeting-house, but after my uncle by that name moved away, it was moved a short distance and called

Bethlehem. It has been fifty-seven years since I joined the church there. I was never happier than I was the day I preached there. I felt that God was with me and it was good to be there. I suppose there were two hundred relatives in the congregation. "How good and how pleasant it is for brethren to dwell together in unity." Lord grant we may meet in heaven, where parting shall be no more. Aunt Drucilla is the widow of David Thompson. Their son James is just my age and is the class-leader at old Bethlehem. They have a camp-ground there, with a very large arbor, and hold their camp-meeting so as to embrace the fourth Sabbath in September annually. Frederick Thompson, the father of Uncle David, was a local preacher. Daniel Clowers, the great oddity of Georgia, was an exhorter in the Methodist Church. He was uncle to Morgan Terrentine, the oldest member of the Alabama Conference, also to General Terrentine of Gadsden, Alabama.

These two old brethren generally held their meetings together. They had an appointment at Brother Thomas Leg's, on Mulberry Creek, in Jackson County, Georgia. The dwelling was a log house. There were pegs driven in the wall to hold a side cupboard, in which they kept their crockery and milk. Uncle Daniel was conducting the service, Uncle Thompson was sitting leaning against the cupboard, and the top of his chair-post had slipped under the bottom of the cupboard. When Father Clowers closed his sermon he called on Brother Thompson to close. He went to rise and lifted the cupboard off the pegs right on top of his head. It spilled the milk all over him and broke all the crockery Brother Leg had. Brother Thompson got down on his knees, picking up the broken pieces of crockery. Brother Clowers exclaimed, "Why, Fed!" The services closed.

Chapter XXI

*I*N those early days the population, with the exception of mechanics, and these were a very small proportion, and the few professional men and country merchants, was entirely agricultural. This rural pursuit confined at home and closely to business every one. Popular meetings were confined to religious gatherings on Sunday in each neighborhood, and the meeting of a few who could spare the time at court in the village county-seat twice a year. There were no places of public resort for dissipation or for amusement. A stern morality was demanded by public opinion of the older members of society. Example and the switch enforced it with the children. Perhaps in no country or community was the maxim of good old Solomon more universally practiced upon, "Spare the rod and spoil the child," than in middle Georgia fifty years ago. Filial obedience and deference to age was the first lesson. "Honor thy father and mother, that thy days may be long on the earth or the land" was familiar to the ears of every child before they lisped the A, B, C, and upon the first demonstration of a refractory disobedience a severe punishment taught them that the law was absolute and inexorable. To lie or touch what was not his own was beyond the pale of pardon or mercy, and a solitary aberration was a stain for life. The mother, clad in home-spun, was chaste in thought and action; unlettered and ignorant, but pure as ether. Her literature confined to the Bible. Its maxims directed her conduct and was the daily lesson of her children.

The Hardshell Baptist was the dominant religion, with here and there a Presbyterian community, generally characterized by superior education and intelligence, with a preacher of so much learning as to be an oracle throughout the land. The Methodists were just then beginning to grow in importance, and their circuit-riders, now fashionably known as itinerants, were passing and preaching, and establishing societies to mark their success through all the rude settlements of the State. These were the pioneers of this truly democratic sect of stern morality and upright bearing, which had so powerful an influence over the then rising population. It is more than sixty-five years since I first listened to the Methodist circuit-riders, among whom was Thomas Sanford, one of the great men of the Georgia Conference, Wm. Arnold, Wm. Parks, Epps and Joshua Tucker, Isaac Oslin, Thomas L. Winn, and Richard his brother, John Howard, Joel Townsend, Anderson Ray, Wm. and Nathan Rhodes, Stegall, Frederick P. Nosworthy, James K. Hodges, Benjamin Pope, Thomas Capers, Thompson Glenn, and his brother. These were itinerants. Among the local preachers were Hosea Camp, Jonathan Betts, Josephus Harrison, William Myers, John Moate, Anderson Frost, James Cook, William Pentecost, Joseph Smith, Frederick Thompson, William Pindergrass, Seth Thomas, Walter T. Colquit, who was judge of the Superior Court and would always open the session of his court with prayer. Colquit represented Georgia in the United States Senate, and I think the greatest man in the State in his day.

Geo. W. Troupe was a man of wonderful powers. During his administration a contest arose as to the true western boundary of the State—on the right of the State to the territory occupied by a portion of the Creek tribe Indians. In the difficulty arising out of the sale by the legislature of the lands belonging to the State bordering upon the Mississippi River a compromise was effected by Congress with the company purchasing, and Georgia had sold to the United States her claim to all the lands in the original grant to General Oglethorpe and others by the English government west of the Chattahoochie River. A part of the consideration was that the United States should, at a convenient time and for the benefit of Georgia, extinguish the title of the Indians and remove them from the territory occupied by them east of the Chattahoochie River to a certain point upon that stream, and from this point east of a line to run from it directly to a point called Neckey Jack, on the Tennessee River. The war of 1812 with Great Britain found the Creek or Alabama portion of this tribe of Indians allies of England. They were by that war conquered and their territory wrested from them. Those of the tribe under the influence of the celebrated chief Wm. McIntosh remained friendly to the United States, and were active in assisting in the conquest of their hostile brethren. The conquered Indians were removed from their territory and homes into the territory east of Line Creek, which was made the western boundary of the Creek nation's territory. Many of them came into the territory claimed by Georgia as her domain. This war was a war of the Republican party of the United States, and the State of Georgia being almost unanimously Republican, her people felt it would be unpatriotic at this juncture to demand of the government the fulfillment of her obligations in removing the Indians from her soil. The expenses of the war were onerous and felt as a heavy burden by the people, and one which was incurred by Republican policy. That party felt that it was its duty to liquidate this war-debt as speedily as possible. To this end, the sale of those conquered lands would greatly contribute, relieving at the same time the people to some extent from the heavy taxation they had borne during the war. Consequently they had not pressed the fulfillment of this contract upon the government. But now the war-debt had been liquidated, the United States treasury was overflowing with surplus treasure, Indian tribes were being removed by the purchase of their lands in the northwest, and a tide of population pouring in upon these lands and threatening a powerful political preponderance in opposition to southern policy and southern interest. Under these circumstances and on the recommendation of Governor Troupe, the legislature of the State, by joint resolution and memorial to Congress, demanded the fulfillment of the contract on the part of the United States and the immediate removal of the Indians. John Quincy Adams was at that time President of the United States, and, as he had ever been, was keenly alive to northern interests and to Federal views. Though professing to be Republican in political faith, he arrayed all his influence in opposition to the rights of the States. In this matter he gave the cold shoulder to Georgia. He did not recommend a repudiation of the contract, but interposed every delay possible to its consummation.

After some time commissioners were appointed to negotiate a treaty with the Indians for the purchase of their claim to the lands within the boundaries established by the sale of the United States, or so much thereof as was in possession of the Creek tribe. To this there was very serious opposition, not only from that portion of the tribe which formerly allied themselves to Great Britain, but also from missionaries found in the Cherokee country and from Colonel John Crowell, who was the United States agent for the Creek Indians. These Indians were controlled by their chief, Hopothlegohola, a man of rare abilities and great daring. He was a powerful speaker, fluent as a fountain and extremely vigorous in his expressions. His imagery was original and beautiful, apposite and illustrative, and his words and manner passionate to wildness. To all this he added the ferocity of his savage nature. Crowell was an especial friend of Governor Clarke and was influenced by his party feelings of hatred to Troupe in his opposition to the treaty, openly declaring that Georgia should never acquire the land while Troupe was Governor. He was an unscrupulous man, of questionable morals and vindictive as a snake. The persevering energy of Troupe, however, prevailed. A treaty was negotiated and signed by Crowell, as agent, and a number of the chiefs headed by McIntosh. No sooner was this done than Crowell, with a number of chiefs, hurried to Washington to protest against the ratification and execution of the treaty, charging the United States commissioners with fraud in negotiating under the influence of Troupe, prompted by W. A. Crawford and friends. The fraud charged was in giving presents to the chiefs and a couple of reservations of land to McIntosh, one where he resided and the other around and including the famous Sulphur Spring, known as the Indian Spring, in Butts County. This habit of giving presents to the chiefs when negotiating treaties has always been the custom of the government. They expect it. It is a part of the consideration paid for the treaty of the sale, for they are universally the vendors of territory and the negotiators of treaties for their tribe. This charge was simply a subterfuge, and one that was known would be influential with the philanthropists of the North, Mr. Adams, and the senators and representatives from New England. On the assumption of fraud based upon these charges alone, the treaty was set aside by the action of the President and Cabinet alone, and by the same authority a new one made with a change of boundary involving a loss of a portion of territory belonging to Georgia under the stipulations of the contract between the State and the United States. The previous or first treaty had been submitted to the United States Senate and duly ratified, thereby becoming a law under which Georgia claimed vested rights.

It was under these trying circumstances that the stern and determined character of Troupe displayed itself. Holding firmly to the doctrine of State rights, he notified the President that he should disregard the latter treaty and proceed to take possession of the territory under the stipulations of the former one. Upon the receipt of this information, General Gaines was ordered to Georgia to take command of the troops stationed along the frontier of the State and any additional troops which might be ordered to this point, with orders to protect the Indians and to prohibit the taking possession of the territory as contemplated by Governor Troupe. A correspondence ensued between General Gaines and Governor Troupe of a most angry character. It terminated with an order to General Gaines to forbear all further communication with the government of Georgia. This was notified to the President:

JOHN QUINCY ADAMS, President of the United States:

Sir—I have ordered General Gaines to forbear all further communication with this government. Should he presume to infringe upon this order I will send your Major General by brevet home to you in irons.

GEORGE M. TROUPE, Governor of Georgia.

The surveyors previously appointed by the legislature were directed to be on the ground, in defiance of United States authority, on the first day of September succeeding, and at sunrise to commence the work of surveying the lands. A collision was anticipated as certain between the troops of the United States and the authorities of Georgia. But there was a difficulty in the way not previously contemplated. Colonels John S. McIntosh, David Emanuel Twiggs, and Duncan Clinch, each commanded regiments in the South. Twiggs and McIntosh were native Georgians, Clinch was a North Carolinian, but was a resident of Florida, Zachary Taylor was the Lieutenant-Colonel of Clinch's regiment. He was a Virginian by birth but resided in Mississippi. All were southern men in feeling as well as by birth, and all Jeffersonian Republicans politically. McIntosh and Twiggs were fanatical in their devotion to the State of their birth. The ancestors of both were among the first settlers and both were identified with her history. The three wrote a joint letter to the President, tendering their commissions if ordered to take arms against Georgia. This letter was placed in the hands of one who was influential with Mr. Adams, to be delivered immediately after the order should be issued to General Gaines to prevent by force of arms the survey ordered by Governor Troupe.

Troupe had classified the militia and signified his intention to carry out if necessary the first negotiated treaty by force of arms as the law of the land. It was unquestionably the prudence of this friend which prevented a collision. He communicated with Mr. Adams confidentially and implored him not to issue the order. He assured him that a collision was inevitable if he did, and caused him to pause and consult his advisors, who declared their conviction that the first treaty was the law of the land, and that Georgia held vested rights under it. In obedience to this advice, Mr. Adams made no further effort to prevent the action of Georgia, and the lands were surveyed and disposed of by the State under and according to the terms of the first treaty, and she retains a large strip of territory that would have been lost to her under the last treaty.

These facts are obtained from Wm. H. Sparks, in "Memories of Fifty Years."

Chapter XXII

The Slave-Trade — The Intentions of Divine Wisdom — John Wesley, the Founder of Methodism — Its Doctrines

*I*T was at this period that the competition for accumulating money may be said to have commenced in middle Georgia. Labor became in very great demand and the people began to look leniently upon the slave-trade. The marching of Africans, directly imported, through the country for sale is a memory of sixty-five years ago. The demand had greatly increased and with this the price. The trade was to cease in 1808, and the number brought over was daily augmenting to hasten to make from the traffic as much money as possible before this time should arrive. The demand, however, was greater than could be supplied. From house to house they were carried for sale. They were always young men and women or girls and boys, and their clothing was of the simplest kind. That of the men and boys consisted of drawers only, reaching midway the thigh from the waist. The upper portion of the person and the lower extremities were entirely nude. The females wore a chemise reaching a few inches below the knee, leaving bare the limbs. This was adopted for the purpose of exposing the person as much as decency would permit for examination, so as to enable the purchaser to determine their individual capacity for labor. This examination was close and universal, beginning with an inspection of the teeth, which in these young savages were always perfect, save in those where they had been filed to a point in front. This was not uncommon with the males. It was then extended to the limbs. They yielded to this inspection without the slightest manifestation of offended modesty. At first they were indifferent to cooked food, and would chase and catch and eat the grasshoppers and lizards with the avidity of wild turkeys, and seemed, as those fowls, to relish these as their natural food. From such is descended the race which our brothers of the North have, in their belief as a duty to God, made masters of our destiny. Our faith in the justice and goodness of the same divine Being bids us believe this unnatural and destructive domination will not be permitted to endure for any lengthy period. Could the curtain which veiled out the future sixty years ago have been lifted, and the vision of those then subduing the land been permitted to pierce and know the present of their posterity, they would have achieved a separation from our puritanical oppressors and built for themselves and their own race, even if in blood, a separate government, and have made it, as nature intended it should be to this favored land, a wise and powerful one. Sooner or later these intentions of divine wisdom are consummated. The fallible nature of man, through ignorance or the foolish indulgence of bad passions in the many, enable the few to delude and control the many and to postpone for a time the inevitable, but assuredly as time endures nature's laws work out natural ends. Generations may pass away, perhaps perish from violence, and others succeed with equally unnatural institutions, making miserable the race, until it, like the precedent, passes from the earth. Yet these great laws work on, and in the end triumph in perfecting the divine will. To the wise and observant, this design of the Creator is ever apparent; to the foolish and the wicked, never.

John Wesley had visited Savannah and traveled through the different settlements then in embryo, teaching the tenets and introducing the simple worship of the church of his founding after a method established by himself, and which gave name and form to the sect known as Methodists. The tenets of its faith were most admirably suited to a rude people, and none perhaps could have been more efficient in forming and improving such morals. Unpretending, simple in form, devoid of show or ceremony, it appealed directly to the pure emotions of our nature, and through the natural devotion of the heart lifted the mind to the contemplation and inspired the soul with the love of God. Its doctrines based upon the purest morality, easily comprehensible, and promising salvation to all who would believe, inspiring an enthusiasm for a pure life, were natural, and naturally soon became widespread, and have done more in breaking away the shackles of ignorance and debasing superstition from the mind than any other system of worship or doctrine of faith taught by man, and to this, in a great degree, is due the freedom of thought, independence of feeling and action, chivalrous bearing, and the high honor of the southern people, inculcating as it does the simple teachings of the Gospel of Christ, to live virtuously, do no wrong, love thy neighbor as thyself, and unto all do as you would be done by;—a teaching easy of comprehension, and which, when firmly enforced by a pure and elevated public sentiment, becomes the rule of conduct, and society is blessed with harmony and the moral power is omnipotent for good, concentrating communities into one without divisions or dissensions, to be wielded for good at once and at all times. Nothing evil can result from such concentration of opinions being directed by the vicious and wicked, so long as the moral of this faith shall control the mind and heart.

Chapter XXIII

*C*AMP-MEETINGS, an institution of this church, and which were first commenced in Georgia, are a tradition there now. Here and there through the country yet remains in ruinous decay the old stand or extemporized pulpit from which the impassioned preacher addressed the assembled multitude of anxious listeners, and around the square now overgrown with brushwood and forest-trees, prostrate and rotten, the remains of the cabin tents may be seen where once the hospitality of the owners and worshipers was dispensed with a heartiness and sincerity peculiar to the simple habits and honest, kindly emotions of a rude and primitive people.

How well do I remember the first of these meetings I ever witnessed. It was about sixty years ago, at a church called Concord, in Jackson County, Ga., near the Jug Tavern, within a few miles of the Indian boundary, which was the Appalachie. The people had plank and board tents. Some stretched tent-cloths, and with the addition of their wagons would make room for their family and friends. At daylight they blew a trumpet all around the line of tents to awaken the people. About sunrise they sounded the trumpet again for prayers in each tent, and at eight o'clock they blew the trumpet at the stand for preaching, also at eleven, three, and at night generally about dark. At the close of every service the minister would invite penitents. At nearly every service more or less would profess to be converted. I have seen a large altar under those brush arbors full of seekers or penitents and have seen them stricken down like dead men. I remember well at this same camp-ground, when I was quite a child, after the sermon at eleven on Sabbath I

went up to the railing of the altar and there lay prostrate on the straw a
well-dressed gentleman apparently dead. He did not breathe at all that I
could see. A child that I was, I said to some one standing by, it's bad times
here. He said, no, it's good times. Conversions in those days were bright
and powerful. Why are they not so now? I have known persons stricken
down and apparently breathless for two or three days at a time. I knew a
Bro. Matson to be perfectly helpless frequently for days. I asked him once
to describe his feelings while in this trance or apparently dead state. He said
he was perfectly sensible to all his surroundings, and that if he could have
spoken could have told me what was going on in New York or any where
else. When he came to his speech he was well and natural as ever.

The arbors of green boughs cut from the adjoining forest formed a shelter
from the sun's rays. Under this friendly sheltering from the heat of the sun
assembled the owners and guests of each in social and unceremonious
intercourse. This was strictly the habit of young people, and here in evening's
twilight has been plighted many a vow which has been redeemed by happy
unions for life's journey, and to be consummated when the cold weather
came. In the rear of the tents were temporary kitchens, which were presided
over in most instances by some old trusted aunty of ebon hue, whose pride it
was to prepare the meals for her tent and to hear her cooking praised by the
preachers and by the less distinguished guests of master and mistress. The
sermons were preached with power and the Holy Ghost. The tenters would
come at the sounding of the horn, leading their families and friends. The
husband with an ample chair of home manufacture slung by his side for his
wife's comfort, as she devoutly listened to the sermon. The guests and young
of the family following in respectful silence, all tending to the great arbor of
bushes covering the place of worship. Over all the space of the encampment
the brush had been carefully removed, but the great forest-trees were always
left to shade as well as they might the pulpit, stand, and grounds. All around
was a dense forest, wild and beautiful as Nature made it. How well the scene
and the worship accorded. There was congruity in all—the woods, the tents,
the people, and the worship. The impressions made that day upon my young
mind were so indelibly impressed as only to pass away with existence. The
preacher arose upon his elevated platform and advancing to the front where
a simple plank, extending from tree to tree before him formed a substitute
for a table or desk, where rested the hymn-book and Bible, commenced the
service by reading a hymn, and then, line by line, repeating it to be sung by

all his congregation. Whoever has listened in such a place, amidst a great multitude, to the singing of that beautiful hymn commencing "Come thou fount of every blessing" by a thousand voices, all in accord, and not felt the spirit of devotion burning in his heart, could scarcely be moved should an angel host rend the blue above him and floating through the ether praise God in song. In that early day of Methodism very few of those licensed to preach were educated men. They read the Bible and expounded its great moral truths as they understood them. Few of them ever knew that it had been in part originally written in the Hebrew tongue and the other portion in that of the Greek, but they knew it contained the promise of salvation and felt that it was their mission to preach and teach this way to their people, relying solely for their power to impress these wonderful truths upon the heart by the inspiration of the Holy Spirit. For this reason the sermons were never studied or written, and their excellence was their fervor and impassioned appeals to the heart and the wild imaginations of the enthusiastic and unlearned of the land.

Genius undisciplined and untutored by education is fetterless and its spontaneous suggestions are naturally and powerfully effective when burning from lips proclaiming the heart's enthusiasm. Thus extemporizing orations almost daily stimulated the mind to active thought, and very many of these illiterate young Methodist preachers in time became splendid orators.

It was the celebrated Charles James Fox who said to a young man just entering Parliament that if he desired to become a great orator, and had the genius and feeling from nature, all he had to do was to speak often and learn to think on his feet. It is to this practice the lawyer and the preacher owe the oratory which distinguishes them above every other class of men. And yet how few of them ever attain to the eminence of finished orators. Eloquence and oratory are by no means identical. One is the attribute of the heart, the other of the head; and eloquence, however unadorned, is always effective, because it is born of the feelings, and there is ever a sympathy between the hearts of men, and the words, however rude and original, which bubble up from the heart freighted with its feelings, rush with electrical force and velocity to the heart and stir to the extent of its capacities. Oratory, however finished, is from the brain, and is but an art. It may convince the mind and captivate the imagination, but never touches the heart nor stirs the soul. To awaken feelings in others, we must feel ourselves. Eloquence is the volume of flame. Oratory the shaft of polished ice. One fires to madness, the other delights and instructs. Religion is the pathos of the heart, and must be awakened from the heart's emotions. The imagination is the great attribute of the mind, gathering and creating thought and inspiring feeling. Hence the peculiar system of the Methodists in their worship is the most efficient in proselytizing, and especially with a rude, imaginative people. The camp-meeting was effectual for this purpose, and its abandonment by our people is as foolish as would be that of a knight who would throw away his sword as he was rushing to battle. Fashion is omnipotent in religion as in other things, and with the more general diffusion of education camp-meetings have come to be considered as common and unfashionable. The masses are in the main illiterate and rude, and it is for the conversion and salvation of the multitudes the preacher should struggle, and in his efforts his most efficient means should be used. The camp-meeting at night, when all the fire-stands are ablaze, and the multitude assembled, and singing is beyond description, when some eloquent and enthusiastic preacher is stimulating to intense excitement the multitude around him with the fervor of his words and the wild, passionate manifestations of his manner, to see the crowd swaying to and fro, to hear the groans and sobs of the half-frenzied multitude, and not infrequently shrieks of joy, all coming up from the half-illuminated spot, is thrillingly exciting. And when the sermon is finished, to hear all this heated mass break forth into songs of wild melody which floats in the stillness of night to the listening ear a mile away in cadences mournfully sweet, makes the camp-meeting among the most exciting of human exhibitions. In such a school were trained those great masters of pulpit oratory, Pierce, Wynans, Capers, and Bascomb. Whitfield was the great exemplar of these, but none perhaps so imitated his style and manner as John Newland Maffit and the wonderful Somerfield.

Like all that is great and enduring, the Methodist Church had its beginning among the humble and lowly. Rocked in the cradle of penury and ignorance, it was firmly fixed in the foundations of society, whence it rose from its own purity of doctrine and simplicity of worship to command the respect, love, and adoption of the highest in the land, and to wield an influence paramount in the destinies of the people. Its ministers are now the educated and eloquent of the church militant. Its institutions of learning are the first and most numerous all over the South, and it has done for female education in the South far more than every other denomination. In the cause of education its zeal is enlisted, and its organization is such as to bring a wonderful power to operate upon the community in every section of the South and West. That this will accomplish much we have only to look to the church to determine. Like the coral insect, they never cease to labor, each comes with his mite and deposits it, and from the humblest beginning this assiduity and contribution builds up great islands in the sea of ignorance, rich in soil, salubrious in climate, and finally triumphant in the conception of the Chief Architect, completing for good the work so humbly begun.

CHAPTER XXIV

*T*HE memories of childhood cling perhaps more tenaciously than those of any other period of life. The attachments and antipathies then formed are more enduring. Our school companions, the children of our immediate neighborhood who first rolled with us upon the grass and dabbled with us in the branch, we never forget. Time, absence, protracted separation, all fail to obliterate the features, the dispositions, or any thing about them which so unconsciously fastens upon the mind and grows into the tender soul of childhood. These memories retain and bring back with them the feelings, the likes and dislikes, which grew with them. These feelings are the basis of lifetime loves and eternal antipathies.

The boy is father to the man and the girl is mother to the woman. Who that has lived seventy years will not attest this from his own life's experience? The generous, truthful boy will be the honorable, noble man. The modest, timid, truthful girl will be the gentle, kind, and upright woman. Nature plants the germ and education but cultivates the tree, it never changes the fruit. The boy who, when dinner-time comes, happens to have a pie and his fellows have none, and will open his basket before his companions and divide with them, will carry the same trait to the grave. His hand will open to assist the needy and he will seek no reward beyond the consciousness of having done right. And he who with the same school-boy's treasure will steal away and devour it behind the school-house alone, will through life be equally mean in all his transactions. From motives of interest, he may assume a generosity of conduct; but the innate selfishness of his heart will in the manner of his dispensing favors betray itself. Education and the influence of polished society may refine the manners, but they never soften the heart to generous emotions where nature has refused to sow its seed. But when her hand has been liberal in this divine dispensation, no misfortune, no want of education or association, will prevent their germination and fructification.

Such hearts divide their joys and sorrows with the unfortunate and afflicted with the same emotional sincerity with which they lift their prayers to Heaven. The school-room is an epitome of the world. There the same passions influence the conduct of the child which will prompt it in riper years, and the natural buddings of the heart spring forth and grow on to maturity with the mind and the person. College-life is but another phase of this great truth, where these natural proclivities are more manifest because more matured. It is not the greatest mind that marks the greatest soul, nor the most successful who are the noblest. The shrewd, the mean, and the selfish grow rich and prosperous, and are courted and preferred, because there are more who are mean and venal in the world than there are who are generous and good, who are the great benefactors of mankind; and yet if there were no selfishness in human nature, there would be no means of doing good.

Wealth is the result of labor and economy. These are not incompatible with generosity and ennobling manliness. The proper discrimination in the application of duties and donations toward the promotion of useful institutions, and the same discrimination in the dispensation of private characters, characterize the wise and good of the world. These attributes of mind and heart are apparent in the child, and in every heart, whatever its character, there is a natural respect and love for these and all who possess them. Such grow with their growth in the world's estimation, and are prominent, however secluded in their way of life or unpretending in their conduct, with all who know them or with whom in the march of life they come in contact. It is to but few that Fortune throws her gifts, and these are rarely the most deserving, or the goddess had not been represented with a bandage over her eyes. She is blind, and though her worshipers are many, she kisses but few, and can not see if they be fair and beautiful or crooked and ugly. Hence most of those who receive her favors conceal them in selfishness and hoard them to be despised, while hundreds slighted of her gifts cultivate the virtues which adorn and ennoble, and are useful and beloved.

Will you who yet live and were children when I was a child, turn back with me in memory to those days and to those who were your school-fellows and playmates then? Do you remember who were the brave and generous, kind and truthful among them, and do you recall their after lives? Were they not the true men in that day?

An exalted intellect, unaccompanied with exalted virtue, can never constitute greatness. In whatever position placed or whatever inducements persuade, virtue and a conscientious conviction of right must regulate the mind and conduct of man to make him great. He whose pedestal is virtue and whose action is honest, secures respect of his own age and becomes the luminary of succeeding ages. Stern honesty often imposes unpleasant duties. Strict obedience to its behests not infrequently involves apparent inconsistencies of conduct, but the conscientious man will disregard these in doing what his judgment determines right—the only real consistency which sustains one in his own estimation and leaves no bitter reflections for the future. To subserve the cause of right is always a duty. All men respect right, but many have not the virtue to resist wrong. Any minnow may float with the current, but it requires a strong fish to stem and progress against the stream. The truly great are only known by nobly resisting every temptation to do wrong and braving the world's condemnation in pursuing and sustaining the right. It is the soul to which greatness belongs, not the mind. The combination of a great mind and a great soul constitutes the truly great, and the life of such a man creates a public sentiment, which like an intense essence permeates all it touches, leaving its fragrance upon all.

Chapter xxv

*A*MONG the great and good was Eli Bynum, of Calhoun County,
Alabama. He was raised in the mountains of Blount, but was one of the
first settlers in Benton, now Calhoun, County; was a man of moderate
means, but rich in faith and the Holy Ghost. He was powerful in prayer.
He lived and died in the same community. For forty-five years he exerted a
hallowed influence on all with whom he had to do. I saw him the day before
he died. He said he was nearing the other shore; that though he had to pass
through the valley and shadow of death, he felt that he had the rod and staff
to support and comfort him. He left a precious wife, two sons, and three
daughters, with many friends to mourn for him. We miss him, especially at
camp and protracted meetings. Even the wicked reverenced him. It seemed
while in his company that you were in the midst of a holy atmosphere. I
never was in his company but I felt that I was benefited. I pray his mantle
may fall upon his children.

I like to think of the precious names with whom I used to worship at
Cold Water—Brothers William and Abram Towns, old father Frank Self,
old father Barr and his sons Colonel Moses and Thomas Barr, Uncle Johnnie
Neighbors, and Harris Taylor. All these brethren worshiped at the same
church. Harris Taylor lived in the community thirty or more years, could get
as large a congregation as any Bishop in the Church, and a song from him
would stir a congregation more than would an ordinary sermon from almost
any other minister, particularly that favorite of his, "One spark, O God, of
heavenly fire." His father was a very poor man. He had three sons—William,
Isaac, and Harris. I doubt if there were three such men in the local ranks of
Alabama. It was listening to William, at the close of a camp-meeting about
forty-seven years since, at Owen's Springs, that I felt and resolved to establish

a family altar, and from that day to this I have had prayers with my family both night and morning, when I was at home and able to do so. Though often it has been quite formal, I find it better to have the form without the power than to have neither form nor power. But thank God, I am not tired of the way yet, and it will not be long until I shall quit the walks of men, and I expect to meet these brethren who have died in the faith and their works have followed them. There are but few with whom I used to worship at Cold Water and Chinnobee who yet linger on this side the river of death. There is but one man—Judge Green T. McAfee—in the city of Talladega who was there when I settled in Chinnobee town, and but few in the county. There still linger Brother Charles Carter, Colonel Thomas McElderry, Reverends John L. and Jacob B. Seay. Charles Carter was originally from Virginia, came to North Alabama at an early day, married there, and has raised a large and interesting family. He yet lives at the place he settled in 1834. He has represented Talladega in the State legislature and made a good member. Colonel McElderry is in his ninety-third year, is still lively and active, usually walks five miles a day over his farm that he settled in 1834. He is quite regular in his habits, consequently has fine health; was raised near Knoxville, Tennessee, and settled in North Alabama at an early day, whence he removed to this portion of the State. He represented Morgan County in the legislature while the capital was at Tuscaloosa. Brother John L. Seay is about my age. His widowed mother also still lingers in her ninety-eighth year. He was originally from Virginia. Being the eldest son, the care of the fatherless family fell upon him, and he has done good part in providing for a widowed mother ever since he was a small boy, also two widowed sisters, for many years. He expects to live long on the earth which the Lord God giveth him, because he has honored his mother. He yet leads her to his table at every meal. We have been intimately associated for forty-eight years, have each raised a large family, and commenced our ministry near the same time. Though I have heard him preach perhaps a thousand times, I still love to hear him talk, as he calls his preaching. Brown (his brother), as we call him, is also a noble spirit.

And now, kind reader, I thank you for following me to the close of my journal. Some of it is sad; but to show you I am happy and glad, and for the benefit of the bachelors and widowers, I will reproduce some verses composed by a Methodist minister, John Howard, for my old bachelor kinsman, and which I learned when I was a boy:

Of all the objects in the world,
Since women first began to scold,
I know of none that looks so sorry
As he who never intends to marry.

He is like a parted pair of scissors,
Or like a broken pair of tweezers—
Of use to none, of pleasure free,
As men of sense will clearly see.

He snaps and snarls, he grunts and groans,
He heaves his sighs and makes his moans;
He's always vexed, he's always sad,
Nor does he like to see one glad.

He stays at home to watch his keys,
While married men, quite at their ease,
Do go abroad their friends to see,
To breakfast, dinner, or to tea.

He eats his morsel all alone;
His tea half made, his bread a pone;
His cup and plate, his knife and fork,
Are always tinged with grease and dirt.

The bed on which he takes repose
Lies in one corner of his house;
His sheets all torn, his blankets black,
And bugs concealed in every crack.

His socks are few and full of holes;
His shoes need mending on the soles;
His breeches are ripped, his shirt all ragged,
His elbows out, his knees are naked.

Sometimes he tries to hide
The evils which I've thus described
By darning socks and patching breeches,
But, alas I with long and ugly stitches.

The stitches, though so far between,
Might pass unnoticed and unseen
If thread and patches matched each other
When they had thus been brought together.

But ofttimes patches black and blue.

Are sewed with thread as white as snow,
Which makes the stitches plainly seen,
Although the patch may hide the skin.
   Now, surely friend, 'tis truly bad
For you to serve that housewife trade,
When God himself this trade designed
Should be pursued by womankind.

THE END

Dr. Peter Bryce. Courtesy of The W.S. Hoole Special Collections Library, The University of Alabama. Bryce Hospital Archives, Box 5976 Folder 0225.02 MSS.0225.

Biographical Note on Peter Bryce

By Robert O. Mellown

*I*N many respects, Peter Bryce (1834–1892) was the ideal superintendent for a moral treatment hospital. By all accounts, he was a man of great charm and character, totally dedicated to his work. His guiding principle was the golden rule: "Above all," he wrote, "do to every patient as you would yourself like to be done by if you were away from home and deprived of your freedom by loss of reason."

Born in Columbia, South Carolina, Bryce attended the Citadel in Charleston and later the University of New York, where he received his medical degree in 1859. Bryce's star rose quickly. Determined to specialize in the treatment of nervous disorders, he went abroad after graduation to study hospitals in Europe. On his return, he became assistant physician at the Insane Hospital in Trenton, New Jersey, the nation's first linear Kirkbride hospital. Hospitals of this type were built according to plans developed by Dr. Thomas Story Kirkbride, America's foremost authority on moral treatment, a reform movement in psychiatry that utilized architectural design and pastoral settings as essential components in the treatment of mental illness. The distinctive plan was characterized by its impressive central pavilion designed to house administrative offices and apartments for the superintendent and his staff of doctors and nurses, and its series of set-back wings located on either side of the central building that were designed to house patients. Segregated by sex and organized by the severity of illness, patients were provided accommodations with the maximum amount of sunlight and air circulation. Kirkbride's plan for hospitals also featured the most advanced indoor plumbing and central heating. Within a few months, Bryce resigned to become first assistant physician at a South Carolina asylum. Six months later, he was offered the post of medical superintendent of the nearly completed Alabama Insane Hospital. Bryce had been recommended for the latter position by Dorothea Dix, who had met him at the Trenton hospital and recognized his potential. On July 1, 1860, he assumed his new post in Tuscaloosa. Before assuming his new position at the Alabama Insane Hospital (another Kirkbride plan structure), the 26-year-old Bryce married his 19-year-old sweetheart, Ellen Clarkson, at her parents' home in Columbia, South Carolina. The young couple took up residence in a third floor apartment in the Center Building of the hospital. Mrs. Bryce played an active role in Tuscaloosa society and in the life of hospital patients. A talented musician, she played the organ at daily religious services and organized music classes and social events for patients.

Bryce's thirty-one-year tenure at the Alabama hospital was filled with challenges that would have defeated a less able administrator. Initially, he faced the problem of completing the enormous hospital on the eve of the Civil War (The first patient, a soldier from Fort Morgan, was admitted in April 1861). Frightened Yankee workmen left for the North, and essential supplies and equipment were cut off by Union blockades.

The moral treatment philosophy proved its worth during this difficult time. The hospital's inmates grew their own food and made most of their own clothes. This state of affairs continued even during Reconstruction when, for a number of years, the hospital received no funds from the bankrupt state. Later, during the 1880s, the ever-increasing numbers of mental patients necessitated costly new construction.

Bryce himself considered his most valuable contribution to the hospital his abolition of mechanical restraints such as straitjackets, bed-straps, and other devices. After ten years of experimenting with this new system, Bryce proudly recorded in his 1889–90 biennial report that "instances have occasionally occurred which to others might have appeared to call for [mechanical restraints]; but in no single case have [the patients] failed in our hands to yield to milder measures."

Dr. Bryce died from Bright's disease on August 14, 1892. At his request, he was buried on the hospital grounds, his grave marked by a simple white obelisk. The following year the Alabama legislature renamed the asylum the Alabama Bryce Insane Hospital, and in 1900 it became simply Bryce Hospital.

Index